Praise for *Writing from the Inside Out*

"Dennis Palumbo's wise, compassionate and funny *Writing from the Inside Out* tells us something that remains a secret in the writing business: Find a subject as a writer that holds your attention so strongly that you forget yourself—and you're already in the money."

—Aram Saroyan, poet and novelist

"Finally, a book that will not only help us become better writers, but better human beings. In *Writing from the Inside Out*, Dennis Palumbo speaks with a wise and authentic voice about the trials and joys of both the writing experience and life itself. Filled with humorous stories and practical, compassionate advice, he feels like the best friend every writer wants and needs. Both a provocative and completely comforting read."

—Earlene Fowler, Agatha-Award-winning author of *Seven Sisters* and *Mariner's Compass*

"Eminently practical advice on how to untangle the mysterious vines of the creative process and successfully continue the journey, and it flashes with that rarest of things—wisdom."

—Richard Setlowe, author, *The Sexual Occupation of Japan* and *The Black Sea*

"In *Writing from the Inside Out*, Dennis Palumbo talks to you, befriends you, gains your trust and then, because he is so convincing and effective, teaches his readers how to capture and become comfortable with the writer's life—the pain, joy, struggle and reward. He is the perfect teacher and companion for a writer in need of support and inspiration."

—Lee Gutkind, editor, *Creative Nonfiction,* and author, *Many Sleepless Nights*

Writing from the Inside Out

Transforming Your Psychological Blocks
to Release the Writer Within

Dennis Palumbo

John Wiley & Sons, Inc.

New York • Chichester • Weinheim • Brisbane • Singapore • Toronto

For
Lynne and Daniel,
with love

ISBN 0-471-38266-3

10 9 8 7 6 5 4 3 2 1

Contents

Contents

Contents

Foreword

Be warned:

This is not a how-to book. It offers nary a rule, formula, nor recipe that will allow you to turn out a best-selling novel or a fabulous, million-dollar screenplay. Just as well. In the end, most million-dollar screenplays turn out to be three-million-dollar screenplays, once the inevitable rewriting frenzy begins and other hands are called in to rescue the formerly fabulous million-dollar screenplay.

It is not that handy-dandy kind of book and that is just as well. Never before have so many of the smugly expert advised so many of the seemingly inexpert on how to write successfully and on how to become rich and anonymous (screen and television writers can reap sizeable financial rewards, but they rarely get anything like famous). The pages that lie ahead provide far more valuable insights and practical tools for the working and/or would-be writer. Instead of a how-to, what Dennis Palumbo has written is a how-come book.

A veteran of the writing wars himself, Palumbo brings fresh insight into the whys and wherefores of the numerous dilemmas each writer faces, or, at times, refuses to admit. He encourages the wanna-bes and the already-ares to confront their concerns, to recognize what lies at the heart of them, to ultimately turn their demons into constructive, liberating collaborators.

The dreaded writer's block? Dennis Palumbo's take on the subject is as novel as it has proved successful for a good number of those who have had the good sense to seek his counseling. What he offers is not a one-size-fits-all cure, but rather an understanding of the sort of writer's speed bump that can sometimes seem the size of a mountain. By leading the sufferer to the underlying truth of his or her particular form of this creative cramp, Palumbo lays the groundwork for a way not around the problem, but one that goes right straight through it.

Procrastination? Doubt? Fear of failure? Loneliness? You name it; Palumbo's been there, done those—in his own writing career and in his artful advice to others. (Even in the act of writing this brief curtain-raiser, I have (1) procrastinated finishing it until the very last second of my deadline, (2) doubted that I was the best choice for this assignment, (3) been dreading how awful it would be to fail, not writing terribly well about this terribly well-written book, and (4) thought how lonely it was today—as it is every working day—to sit down in my solitary room without one person there to say "good morning" to me.)

For years, I was convinced that I could not write alone, that I needed a partner or to work as a member of a staff, surrounded by multiple partners. I had no faith in my ability to produce material on my own. What this wise, accessible volume makes crystal clear is that no one writes alone, that our superficial appearance merely represents the outer limits of the complex, teeming population that resides in each of us: the brave, the fearful, the confident, the unsure—the braggart worrier who sits not beside but within anyone with the temerity to pan for the gold that lies hidden in the blank page or the monitor.

Early on, Palumbo promotes the concept of the Buddy System, the idea that every writer needs someone who has gone through what you're going through; someone who is happy to serve as an ear, a shoulder, a kindred spirit. Some-one who gets it: the work you're doing, the town or medium in which or for whom you're doing it, someone who has been to the same meetings, been given the same notes by executives, stars, directors, editors, whoever (probably word for word the very same notes you were given by someone else about a totally different piece of work). Most impor-tantly, you need to get someone who gets you. Dennis Palumbo's *Writing from the Inside Out,* with Dennis serving as a thoroughly knowledgeable, compassionate companion, makes him not only a useful friend but one who is user-friendly as well. He is the buddy every writer dreams about—that is, if writer's block isn't keeping you up all night.

Larry Gelbart

Acknowledgments

The author would like to thank the following people, without whose help and encouragement this book could not have been written:

Lisa Chambers and Richard Stayton, editors of *Written By*, the magazine of the Writers Guild of America, in which much of this material first appeared;

David Gorton, Ph.D., Bernard Brickman, M.D., and Jeffrey Trop, M.D., for their support and insight;

Robert Stolorow, Ph.D., and the members of the Thursday night consultation group, for helping to make me a better therapist;

Chris Jackson, Don Maass, and Stu Robinson, for their professionalism and guidance;

Neill Hicks, for the title to Part Five;

And to all my friends and colleagues, including Fred Golan, Mark Baker, Richard Setlowe, Linda Marsa, Hoyt Hilsman,

Acknowledgments

Peter Levitt, Michael Parth, Linda Venis, Mark Schorr, Bill Shick, Susan Pembroke, David Levy, Lee Gutkind, Blayne Phillips, Jim Carolla, Darryl Hickman, Lolita Sapriel, Al Hutter, and many others, with my sincere appreciation and gratitude.

Introduction

It's 1978. I'm in a tiny cabin off the beach in Carmel, California, and I'm literally about to bang my head against the wall.

I've been here almost a week, having sequestered myself in this single room, six hours north of my home in Los Angeles, to write a screenplay, my first. The deal's been made, the producer and studio anxiously await the first draft. Four years, a different studio, countless drafts (by myself *and* an additional writer), and dozens of ego-wrenching creative clashes later, the finished film, called *My Favorite Year*, will be released.

But that's a long way off, down a road I can't even see. Right now, in this lonely cabin, whose "rustic" charm has long since faded, there's no big Hollywood movie. There's not even a script. There are only eleven or twelve bad pages, strewn about the room, two wastebaskets filled with crumpled paper—and me.

My head hurts. My shoulders ache. I pace back and forth, rereading the same dozen pages—

Which, not surprisingly, doesn't make them any better.

I have to face it: I'm blocked. Stuck. Hate every word I've written, and have no idea how to make myself write any more.

I glance at the desk clock. Another twenty minutes gone. Lost. *Wasted.*

The electric typewriter's hum has gotten louder, as if with growing impatience. But I don't dare shut it off. What if I never turn it back on again?

Finally, filled with equal parts shame and self-pity—has *anyone* suffered so much?—I bolt from the cabin, telling myself I need fresh air. The beach is just beyond, latticed with shadows as the sun begins to dip.

A walk on the beach. *Perfect,* I think. Outdoors. A change of scene. Just the thing to clear my mind, get the gears working again.

And, thankfully, no tempting walls to bang my head against.

Writer's block. Procrastination. Loneliness. Doubt. Fear of failure. Fear of rejection. Just plain . . . fear.

What do these all mean? What does it say about you if you struggle with these feelings on a daily basis?

It's means you're a writer. And that's *all* it means.

I ought to know. I've been a successful writer for over twenty years, and I've spent more than my share of time grappling with most of these feelings.

Now, as a psychotherapist specializing in creative issues, I work with new, struggling writers, as well as some of the most successful in the country. Screenwriters, novelists, TV writers, journalists. From the unknown to the famous, from the unpublished and not yet produced to the long established and award winning. And what do they all have in common?

See above.

The problem is, most writers don't believe this. What they *do* believe is that if they just read the right how-to book, took enough writing seminars, got the best therapy, etc., they could get rid of their doubts and fears, their "negative" feelings and behaviors.

Or, as one of my writer clients expressed it, "I want to just shove all my anxieties, that pain and fear, all that *crap* out the door. Then I could sit down and write."

But write about *what?* Those very feelings we yearn to dispel are the raw materials of our writing, the stuff from which everything we write—including even our desire *to* write—emerges. Rather than shoving them out the door, like unwanted guests who are wrecking the party, I say invite them in. They *are* the party. Or, rather, there's no party without them.

Most how-to books, workshops, and tapes promise to rid you of "negative" behaviors, to impart tips, tricks, and techniques to help overcome your personal defects so you can write. Intentionally or not, they validate the belief that *who you are* is not enough. That there's some *other* way you need to be, some improved version of yourself you need to become.

Which is why I've written this book. If there's one principle that guides my work with writers, one message I fervently want to impress upon you, it's that *you*—everything you are, all your feelings, hopes and dreads, fears and fantasies—*you are enough.*

And, further, that all good writing starts from where you are now.

Which brings me back to that cabin in Carmel.

It's two days later, and I'm still nowhere with the script. The cabin just feels like a jail cell. I *could* walk on the beach again, except I now hate the beach.

I've accumulated even more crumpled paper, scenes begun and halted; begun again and then pulled angrily from the typewriter. Page after page wadded into a ball, then tossed through the opened window into a trash dumpster repositioned there for just this purpose. I'm getting quite accurate at this. Over-the-shoulder tosses. Left- or right-handed. Eyes closed. Shoots. Scores!

The dumpster slowly fills with paper. Trees have died in vain.

I'm beginning, I think, to panic.

I feel foolish, stupid, anxious that I've led people to expect something from me that I can't deliver. Like I often felt as a kid.

Just like when I was a kid. I can almost see that kid, right here and now in the cabin. I can *see* him, sitting on the edge of the bed, feeling deflated. Ashamed.

I wish I could rescue him. I wish *someone* could. A hero. Like in the movies.

This brings another image to mind. And now I smile. After all, it was the thing that had given me the idea for the movie in the first place.

It was back in Pittsburgh, and I was an adolescent listening to my Dad talk about Errol Flynn, his favorite movie star. This was in the late 1950s and early 1960s, when you could still see old movies on the *Late Show.*

I remember how often my father would sneak into my bedroom to wake me at some ungodly hour and get me up to join him in the living room. There, we'd press our faces against the TV screen so we could hear—the volume was barely audible, so we wouldn't wake Mom and catch hell; after all, it *was* a school night! There, on the old Magnavox, we'd watch Errol Flynn in *The Adventures of Robin Hood* or *The Sea Hawk.*

As I sit in the cabin now, tears form in my eyes: so many memories of my childhood, and movies, and my father communicating with me the only way he knew how; a kaleidoscope of yearnings, failings, ups and downs, hero worship versus reality.

I see, with sudden clarity, what the screenplay is actually *about.*

Then, abruptly, my memories shift to just last year, in L.A., and my first actual writing job, on the ABC sitcom *Welcome Back, Kotter.* I was twenty-five years old, one of the new kids on the staff, which was just as exciting and terrifying as it sounds: learning to write, dealing with office politics, desperate for models, mentors, saviors.

Just as the lead character in my movie is the new kid on staff at the 1950s variety show *he's* working on, the one whose guest star that week is a matinee idol modeled after Errol Flynn. . . .

I see again, as memory fragments cluster in my mind, as my yearnings from childhood and my experiences on the sitcom's writing staff weave together, what the screenplay is all about.

5

And now, the cabin is no longer a cell, no longer lonely. It's crowded with memory, feelings, regrets and hopes, people, places, events; and my sudden, urgent desire to get this all *down*.

So I begin typing, still in fits and starts, still as unfocused and unformed as the roughest first draft.

But I'm writing.

And the more I mine the emotional landscape of my *own life*, the more I risk allowing the myriad feelings, ideas, and enthusiasms to emerge, the more I trust the raw materials of my inner world, the better it gets.

This is not a how-to book for writers, in the sense of promising to help you write that best-selling novel or Oscar-winning screenplay. It's an attempt to acknowledge and address the real emotions that writers live with every day. It's about winning the "inner game" of writing, if you will; how to thrive in—and not just survive—the writer's life.

From my years as a screenwriter and novelist, and the past decade's experience as a therapist working with writers, I'll try to illuminate and explore some of the underlying issues involved with writing:

That which keeps us from writing versus that which compels us to write;

My belief that we, as writers, need to embrace the very things that so many books and workshops urge us to deny or overcome;

That rather than try to dispel our sometimes contradictory, often painful inner feelings, the goal is awareness and self-acceptance;

How we might better learn to coexist with the *entire* range
of feelings we experience as writers;

And, ultimately, how to challenge the shaming and self-
defeating *meanings* we give to our negative writing experiences, such as

"If I'm stuck, I'm not a real writer."

"If I can't figure out the ending, it means my idea must
be lousy."

"Successful writers don't get anxious about their work,
so there must be something wrong with me."

"If this story gets rejected, it means my family was right
about me all along."

It's only by knowing who we are, and accepting this with
compassion, that we grow as people—*and* as writers. Moreover, if some feeling, painful or not, is in *us,* then it's in our
readers, our audience. The investigation and acceptance of
our authentic experience, and our willingness to write from
that place, are what make the end result compelling, funny,
true.

I'm taught this lesson every day by the clients with whom
I'm privileged to work. Their courage, humor, and perseverance—often against powerful forces either within themselves or in the marketplace—are an inspiration to me. Their
stories, while disguised or amalgamated in these pages to
protect confidentiality, are nonetheless accurate testimony
to the enduring struggle and triumph of the artistic life.

I hope this book does service to them, and to all those
embarking—for the first time or the hundredth—on the
writer's journey.

Part One

THE WRITING LIFE

A writer is someone for whom writing is more difficult than it is for other people.

—THOMAS MANN

Many years ago, I spent an extended period of time in a small town in Massachusetts. As always, I found the New England countryside both exhilarating and soul soothing. Especially in the fall, when the leaves have turned, the air has a snap to it, and the sloping hills seem as old and untroubled as sleeping monks, downy-soft foliage gathered about their shoulders like holy robes.

I spent almost every morning of that vacation walking along quiet dirt roads, past old farm houses and barns, and across ancient covered bridges. Soon I found a favorite spot, near a pond fed by a brisk-moving creek. There stood an old, venerable water-wheel, ceaselessly turning, weathered beams creaking. Water sluiced down a valley formed by twin two-by-fours, quickly filling buckets that hung from rusty wire mesh. I became fascinated by the water-wheel's repetitive toil, the slow, steady orbit of its wooden spokes, the

11

soothing sound of the water that propelled it. It must have been a hundred years old, and yet still did its work.

During my daily visits, that water-wheel came to symbolize something for me, some notion of constancy, purpose, the wheel of life in its unending journey back to itself.

Many times since then, in my work as a writer and therapist, I've thought about that water-wheel and its significance as a metaphor for the writing life. I've thought about the lessons it has to teach about longevity and the virtues of constancy and craft; perhaps, too, about how sound construction and clearness of purpose transcend the vagaries of fads and fortunes.

What constitutes a writer's life? That depends on the writer. There are as many ways to shape and maintain a writing life as there are writers themselves. Some writers work full-time at their craft, either indifferent to or unhampered by financial concerns. Many writers teach, or hold down a succession of day jobs to support their writing. The poet Wallace Stevens famously retained his job as vice-president of the Hartford Insurance Company throughout his notable career.

However you envision your writing life, whatever compromises and sacrifices you make to sustain it, you share with every other writer similar concerns, problems, and frustrations. Hopefully, you also share in the particular joys, both personal and professional, that a dedication to writing can bring.

In this first part of the book, I'd like to talk about some common aspects of the writing life, the kinds of issues and concerns most writers face, and perhaps offer you a new way of thinking about them.

Not quick fixes. Not solutions. Just a different way of thinking that treats you and your struggles at writing with compassion, hope, and the sure knowledge that you're not alone.

This could take some time. I see this part, like the book itself, as a journey, similar to the one each writer undertakes, wherein understanding accumulates, wherein true awareness emerges from experience, wherein things in general go deeper, not faster.

Which brings me back, I guess, to that old water-wheel, and to that one morning, toward the end of my stay, when I watched it operate for a full ten minutes before finally understanding how it worked. That it's not the velocity, but the weight of the water in each bucket, that turns the wheel.

Writer's Block

My new client sat slumped in his chair, face drawn and tired. "I'm here because . . . well, dammit, nothing's coming. . . . Not a page, not a line. . . . I'm totally blocked!"

I nodded sympathetically. But it took everything I had not to extend my hand and say, "Congratulations!"

Let me explain. After all, prior to becoming a therapist, I spent almost twenty years as a screenwriter. I know all too well the maddening frustration of writer's block: I've endured the sleepless nights, the emotional and intellectual fatigue, the insidious undermining of creative confidence. If someone had tried to tell me back then that all this was good news for my writing, I'd have decked him.

And yet, in a way, someone did. I was on assignment from a major studio—an adaptation of a difficult novel by a famous author, and trying to make it work as a linear screen story was twisting me in knots. Page after page, scene after scene ended up in the wastebasket. I felt that old familiar feeling, the one I mentioned earlier: namely, like I was banging my head against a wall.

And then I had a very particular, very vivid dream. (Given how disturbed my sleep was at the time, I'm amazed I hit REM long enough to have one, but I did.) In this dream, I was standing in a broad field while an old-fashioned biplane buzzed me from the air. The famous novelist was leaning out of the plane, gesturing toward the rope ladder that swung from beneath it. He yelled for me to grab the end; all I had to do was jump up and reach for it, but my feet were planted on the ground. All I kept thinking was, *I can't reach, it's too high, I can't. . . .*

When I woke up, I knew immediately why I was stuck on the screenplay.

I had so much respect for the author, I felt unworthy to adapt his novel. As long as I felt this way, I couldn't do what I needed to do—discard much of the middle of the book and totally remake the material for the screen. Which would make it mine.

The problem, I realized, wasn't with the story. The problem was my relationship with myself as a writer. *Who did I think I was, anyway?* That seemed to be the question. As I struggled to answer it, a funny thing happened with the script. The words started coming again.

That was many years ago, but I never forgot it. Since then, as a therapist, I've worked with literally hundreds of writers struggling with writer's block, and I've begun to conceptualize it differently.

For one thing, there's the semantic problem. Calling it a block invites writers to break through or overcome something—something obviously negative—that's impeding the forward momentum of the writing. But if our first impulse upon encountering something is to break through it, we forfeit the opportunity to examine it, to find out what, in fact, it is.

In other words, maybe we should stop banging our heads against the wall long enough to see if it really *is* a wall.

What if, instead, "writer's block" is a signpost, a harbinger of an impending transition or passage (kind of like the monolith that keeps appearing in *2001: A Space Odyssey*)? If we think of our writing skill as a fluid, dynamic thing that grows in subtlety and depth as we gain in experience and self-trust, isn't it possible that what feels like a block is instead the balled-up tension presaging another growth spurt?

Imagine it like this: You, the writer, stand on one plateau, staring across a chasm at another plateau at a slightly higher elevation. You want to make that creative leap to the next plateau, but your fears and doubts hold you back. No longer satisfied on the lower plateau, but not quite able to make the jump to the next, you're frozen in midleap, in the tension between where you've been and where you're going.

What exists in that tension—old beliefs, self-concepts, past writing experiences, etc.—is what needs to be explored and understood. For example, perhaps you're afraid to discover, if you were to complete your writing project, that you're not as gifted as you'd hoped. And that this would confirm your life-long fear that your goals will always exceed your talent. Some perceived inadequacy or defect might become revealed, exposing you to shameful self-recrimination. Is it any wonder, in the face of such fears (conscious or otherwise), you'd stay frozen on that lower plateau?

Thinking about it this way, you might be able to see the block for what it is: a self-protective mechanism, one probably "installed" in your childhood, that's continuing on in your adult life. The same risks of self-exposure, of shame and potential humiliation, that might have been present in your early years may well reemerge as you try to write. And that same defense mechanism you learned as a child—shutting down emotionally, suppressing your natural creative expansiveness—will also reemerge. Only you'll call it writer's block.

Here's another example, from my private practice: I once had a novelist client whose block, when we finally were able to understand it, had a very specific function: Throughout my client's childhood, his Socialist father raged against all authority figures, the "big shots" who kept the little guy down. Now, as a writer whose work was slowly bringing him some recognition, my client had feelings of anxiety and dread; at a level below his conscious awareness, some part of him felt he would betray his late father's ideals by becoming too successful, by becoming a big shot, one of those men for whom his father had nothing but contempt. For this writer, being blocked was a way to forestall this; if he couldn't finish his work, he wouldn't become rich and famous, thus severing a deeply felt tie with his beloved father.

Invariably, once a writer fully experiences and integrates the lessons a block has to teach, his or her work deepens in richness, emotional truth, and, often, personal relevancy. Moreover, the next time such a block appears, the tools are available to explore it, understand it, and work through it until the writing starts flowing again. And another plateau has been reached.

So give yourself a break. You *can* get there from here, not *despite* your writer's block, but *because* of it. It means you're ready—or, probably, more than ready—to make that important next step in your writing.

And that sounds like good news to me.

Your "Baby"

I'm often asked what my main goal is when working with creative clients. Of course, this question has many answers, depending on what issues my client brings into the therapy session. But among the myriad goals, both professional and personal, that we strive to address in our work together, one salient concern seems to emerge: that the client develop a benign relationship with his or her talent.

What do I mean by this? To answer, let me ask a question: Do you treat your craft, your writing talent, the way you were treated as a child?

For example, if you were subject to intense criticism and judgment as a child, are you as critical and demanding of your writing?

Or maybe your parents needed you to be the perfect little boy or girl, to not make any mistakes. Do you subject your writing to the same conditions? As parents often need a child to be perfect to enhance and maintain good feelings about themselves, do you require perfection from your writing to validate you?

I'm often struck, in session with clients, at their displays of rage, disgust, and disappointment with their work. As though, if they could just threaten, or cajole, or reason with their writing talent, it would come around in some way.

I once had a client, frustrated with new pages of a novel she was writing, bring them into my office just so she could tear them into pieces in front of me. She hated her work and what she felt it "said" about her.

As we explored her feelings, what emerged was the memory of countless caustic, disdainful outbursts from her father, who made it quite plain how disappointed he was in her. Now, as an adult, the meaning she gave to her own work when it disappointed her was that it exhibited the same unworthiness as she apparently had, and deserved nothing less than her contempt.

What got me thinking along these lines was something that happened to me many years ago. Driving home from a party, I realized I'd left my best jacket back at the home of my host. Angry with myself, I turned around and headed back, the whole time cursing myself under my breath for my stupidity and forgetfulness. You'd have thought I'd committed the crime of the century. Over a jacket, for God's sake.

Then suddenly I stopped, as though hearing myself for the first time. I imagined myself at six years old, sitting in the seat next to me, and that the child had left his jacket at the party, and I'd been speaking this way to him. The angry, shaming words turned to ashes in my mouth.

I never forgot that moment, and I see it played out in

similar fashion every day in my practice: writers who berate their talent when it doesn't perform up to their expectations, writers locked in an antagonistic, adversarial dynamic with the "child" that is their writing.

Ironically enough, these same writers often refer to their novel or screenplay as their "baby." Except, who the hell would treat a baby the way they treat their work?

If your six-year-old came to you with a drawing he did in art class, would you respond by saying, "You call that a picture? If that's the best you can do, maybe you ought to think of another line of work. And, besides, how do you think it makes *me* feel, having a kid who draws so badly? I'm embarrassed to call you mine."

How enthusiastic do you think that six-year-old would be about showing his next piece of work to you?

The preceding scene sounds ridiculous, of course, and unbelievable—but many writers engage in a similar interior dialogue with their work every day.

This brings me back to what I believe is a fundamental goal for every writer: to develop a benign relationship with his or her talent.

As a writer begins to accept and trust himself or herself, it becomes easier to accept and trust the writing that emerges and see what it has to teach, no matter what he or she thinks of it. Like a loved and valued child, the work will have the freedom to explore, risk, make mistakes, take wrong turns, whatever.

And for you, the writer, every scene, every page doesn't become your life and your death, the determiner of how okay you can feel about yourself that day.

Ultimately—like a caring, supportive parent who's pleased

merely because the child drew a picture at all—for the writer a good scene becomes one you write, a good story one you finish.

And a good day at the word processor is one where you just show up and do it.

Inspiration

One of my favorite moments in Neil Simon's play *The Odd Couple* occurs when Oscar invites the Pigeon Sisters down for dinner, and a reluctant Felix is trying to make conversation with the ebullient young women. Asked what he does for a living, Felix tells them he writes the news.

"Really?" says a Pigeon. "Where do you get your ideas?"

Most writers know this question, having been asked it by friends, family, casual acquaintances, and every repair person who visits the house. Getting "the idea," or the inspiration to tell a story, is part of the lore of writing, the mythology of literary creation.

When asked how she got the idea for *Harvey,* playwright Mary Chase replied, "I looked up from the breakfast table one morning, and there he was."

This is the kind of story that can give new (and not so new) writers an anxiety attack: the belief that a million-dollar idea just "comes to you," that the lucky few are visited by the spirit of creativity and originality. Even Shakespeare, in his prologue to *Henry V,* implores the gods to inspire him: "O for a Muse of Fire, that would ascend the brightest heaven of invention—"

Most of us, when having breakfast, rarely encounter an invisible six-foot rabbit. Or a Muse of Fire, for that matter. We encounter the blank page, the empty computer screen.

The idea of "inspiration," as it's commonly understood, does a great deal of damage to writers. For one thing, it devalues *craft,* which I think is the most important part of writing. It also, as I've cautioned before, reinforces the notion that the writer himself or herself is somehow not enough. That some special talent or knowledge or divine gift—something outside of the writer—is necessary.

What makes any discussion of inspiration so difficult is that writing is such a special, intangible, fragile process—and, at the same time, a demanding, back-breaking, often unforgiving task.

Inspiration, by its very nature, cannot be grasped or looked for, and certainly not commanded to show up. It emerges, unbidden; embedded, I believe, in the deepening layers of craft a writer develops.

I often recommend a book by George Leonard called *Mastery* to my writer clients. It's a short, simple defense of the concept of "practice," of craft for its own sake. Leonard contends that the peaks of achievement, whether in the arts, sports, or any area of endeavor, come from a love of the day-to-day practice of the thing. Because the truth is, in any consistent endeavor, you spend most of the time not on the peaks but on the level ground, where you rarely see any noticeable improvement. If you just live for, or get pleasure from, the peaks, you never grow. Love the craft, the practice of your art, and the peaks will come.

I conceptualize inspiration in the same way. Learn the writer's craft, write regularly, grow to love the practice for its own sake—and inspiration will either come on a particular day or it won't, but you'll have prepared the way for it.

The professional writer, the true craftsperson, understands the pragmatic wisdom of Leonard's advice. As Albert Morovia said, "I pray for inspiration . . . but I work at the typewriter four hours a day."

That's fine, you may be saying. If you're a poet or a songwriter. But what about writing that has deadlines, impatient producers, that has to meet the sometimes formulaic demands of film and television?

Okay, let's look specifically at screenwriting. Though in many ways perhaps the most pragmatic of literary tasks, even it lends itself well to this approach. As your craft attains depth and consistency, as you master the tools of storytelling and character, you create an environment available to the nuances of inspiration—even within the strict narrative and commercial confines of the form.

Moreover, you may develop, as Leonard suggests, the understanding that the true love of something comes from the doing of it, not from its more obvious fruits. As one of my clients put it at the end of a long personal struggle to accept the ups and downs of his writing career, "Love the process, not the pay-off."

Given the shifting winds of fortune that accompany any writer's life, the smart money is on craft, practice, the doing of the thing.

If inspiration shows up, so much the better.

The Buddy System

At the end of Arthur Conan Doyle's *The Sign of Four,* Dr. Watson announces to Sherlock Holmes that he's decided to get married. "Honestly, I cannot congratulate you," Holmes replies, in his usual sharp-edged manner. He then tells Watson quite bluntly that all the marriage means to him is that he's losing a partner.

I'm reminded of that scene from the novel because of something similar that happened recently to one of my writer clients. His best friend, also a writer, had just announced that he was moving back East to work in another business. Though these two were not writing partners, they'd met here in Los Angeles years ago, become friends, and had taken turns supporting each other's careers. For my client, his friend's upcoming move was a devastating loss.

"He was that one guy I could call up at 1 A.M.," my client explained. "The one you could bitch to about anything in this business, and he'd know exactly what you were talking about. The one you could always count on to be on your

26

side, who never lied to you—except those times when you needed a comforting lie, if you know what I mean."

I know exactly what he means. It's what every writer really needs, maybe more than an agent, a computer, or even a shrink. What every writer needs is a buddy.

Remember the buddy system? When we were kids in swimming class, we were always advised to swim with a buddy. When teachers lead school kids across the street, isn't each child instructed to hold hands with another child?

The buddy system recognizes the need for support in navigating new developmental stages or mastering new physical skills. Even as adults, we acknowledge the need for this kind of help when learning a new task. Scuba instructors require that students dive with a buddy. The same goes for learning to rock climb, skydive, a whole range of sports.

Even when it's not officially named as such, the buddy system helps us get through the thornier patches in life. In high school, what is double-dating but an excuse to do a new, frightening social event with the security of a friend having to go through it with you? The same holds true for politics. When attempting to reach the highest office in the land, every presidential candidate has a running mate. A constitutional requirement? Maybe. I say it's the buddy system in action.

In Hollywood—perhaps, next to politics, the thorniest patch of all—writers I know seem to gravitate naturally toward a buddy. This is usually, but not always, another writer; someone who understands the vocabulary of the town, the particular joys and pains of pitch meetings, rewrites, and development deals.

Someone who, to put it simply, gets it. And, more important, gets *you*.

When I was a screenwriter, my best friend—a writer and director—performed this service for me, as I did for him. We'd call each other after bad meetings, replaying the events and offering encouragement. He was the only one I'd let read an unfinished script I was struggling with, confident that he'd be incisive and supportive in just the right measures. He knew my writing style and sensibilities so well, he'd know exactly where I was trying to go with the script— often, before *I* did. And, according to him, this was something I was able to provide him as well.

Though they may not think of it in terms of a buddy system, most of my writer clients have this same kind of relationship with at least one other person in their lives. The one friend who offers clarity in difficult, confusing situations. The one person who tells you when you're "way outta line." The one whose "bullshit indicator" you trust completely. The one you *can* call at 1 A.M. The one person in an often wrenching, contradictory, heart-breaking business that helps you feel less alone.

Agents come and go. So do assignments, good ideas, flush times, and lean times. But for a writer, the buddy system— the long-term, ongoing relationship with that one intellectual, emotional, creative soul mate—is a treasured constant.

It's Alive!

Earlier, I suggested that writers need to develop a benign, fluid, mutually sustaining relationship between themselves and their writing process. Instead, writers often think of their work as a disappointing child to be shamed or bullied into performing, a hunk of stubborn matter to be beaten into shape, a recalcitrant creature to be broken into dutiful (and respectable) profitability.

Certainly the marketplace reinforces this notion. Films, television, and published fiction have never been so derivative and premise driven. Each new movie, new novel, new TV series is more high-concept than the last. The goal-oriented requirement to hammer the chaotic impulses, yearnings, and half-formed ideas in your head into saleable product has never been more intense. To think otherwise is to seem unrealistic, a dreamer, a fool.

Or, worse, an artist.

The problem is, such success in the marketplace—while desirable within its own context—can't be achieved by simple will. Writing that produces prose that people want to read and film footage that people want to see emerges from the irreducible, personal aspects of the writer's interior life. (And all the how-to books and writing software in the world cannot alter this fact.)

In other words, to the extent that you view your writing as a living thing, a process by which you are engaged in a kind of moment-to-moment dialogue of discovery and reflection, this is the extent to which you have a chance to produce vivid work, work that people respond to, work that sells.

The idea of the writing process as a dialogue, an interactive exchange between artist and artifact, is not new. Recently, author and academic Robert Grudin, in his book *On Dialogue: An Essay in Free Thought,* expressed the concept quite well: "The moment you have committed a sentence to paper, the paper declaims that sentence back to you, as another person might. The assembled letters on the page are other than you: yours, yet not wholly yours, for by writing them in language you have entered a forum that is shared by your whole culture. As your manuscript grows, your relationship with it becomes more complex. . . . You may assert that it is under your control, but you forget the controls it exerts on you: The fact that as a writer you are simultaneously a reader, being pulled and pushed by what you have done."

What Grudin underscores here is writing as a living thing, a dialogic process, in which you and your writing create together that which is being written. Until, at some point familiar to all writers, you might come to a scene where a character—call him Bob—is to say or do something, and you stop, thwarted, because you know Bob wouldn't say or do that. The character has taken on a life real enough to conflict with your carefully predetermined plans for him. As temporarily inconvenient as this might be, the smart writer knows this is a good thing. It means the work is alive.

That, ultimately, is the writer's risk, and paradox. To succeed in the marketplace, he or she has to risk setting aside marketplace concerns long enough to stay engaged in organic contact with the writing process in all its permutations, its myriad enthusiasms and disappointments. Which is what makes it such an exciting, terrifying, and amazing business, and not for the faint of heart.

As Grudin says, "You cannot package and distribute living ideas. You cannot manage them; *they* manage you. To interact with living ideas you need a mode of understanding, a method of interpretation, that is open, generous, forgiving, unpunctuated." In other words, like dialogue at its best— free, spontaneous, deepening in insight and imagination.

Just as this kind of interaction with another person informs, enlightens, and emboldens us, so can a sense of our writing process as an ongoing dialogue between ourselves and our work keep it fresh, alive, and potentially compelling to others.

More important, conceptualized this way, our work process contributes to our growth both as writers and people.

To put it another way (and giving Grudin the last word), "If my relationship with a text is dynamic enough, I am rewritten by what I write."

Your "Precious Darlings"

Every writer has them—those great lines of dialogue, that particularly vivid descriptive passage, the one stubbornly insistent joke that never fails to crack you up whenever you insert it into a scene, whether it belongs there or not.

I'm talking about what William Faulkner called a writer's "precious darlings," those favorite phrases or sentences or even whole scenes that—no matter how well written, how ground breaking, how personally aggrandizing—simply don't work in the piece you're writing. They're either repetitive, or beside the point, or distract from the tone and/or narrative flow of the story. For whatever reason, they've got to go. Blue-penciled out. In Faulkner's famous advice, you've got to "kill" them.

But, boy, they die hard! I remember, during my years as a TV writer, one joke in particular that I just loved. I originally wrote it for an episode of the ABC series *Welcome Back, Kotter.* It didn't get past the first rewrite. I resuscitated it again for a screenplay I did a few years later. The producer hated it, and out it went. I swear, for the next ten years or so, I tried to shoe-horn the damn thing into almost every script I wrote. It was like the Flying Dutchman, the *Brigadoon* of jokes that kept reappearing out of the mists. The Joke That Wouldn't Die.

Even *I* knew, after typing it in (and crossing it out) over a dozen times, that there was something perverse in my continuing to try to make use of it. Yes, I thought it was funny—though, now that I recall, it wasn't *that* funny. But there was something else going on . . . and it wasn't until recently that it occurred to me what it might be.

A writer client of mine was describing a descriptive passage she really loved, one that she'd used in a number of short stories (whose editors had deleted it), and that she was determined to use again in a novel she was writing. As we explored her seeming unwillingness to discard this precious darling, we discovered that a number of deeply felt meanings were associated with this particular piece of writing. In her mind, it was the first "strikingly original" (her words) description she'd written, the first that made her feel less derivative of the writers she'd always admired; the first thing she'd written, in fact, that made her feel "like a real writer." Given these powerful feelings of validation for both her craft and ambition, was it any wonder she'd be loathe to "abandon" the words that had provided it?

As I thought about this, I came to understand why writers often report the need to continue submitting magazine stories that have been repeatedly rejected, or pitching the same movie or TV series idea year after year, despite having failed to find a buyer. The meaning these particular stories or ideas have for these writers lies much deeper than their artistic worth: It has to do with the associations the writer makes with them. Maybe it was the first comedy the writer came up with, confirming that he or she indeed was capable of doing so. Maybe the novel represented the first time the writer revealed some intensely personal aspect of his or her own life, and a sense of loyalty to doing so keeps the writer steadfastly committed to seeing it published.

Even in my case, with the Joke That Wouldn't Die, I finally found a hint of the underlying cause of my apparent unwillingness to just let it go. Thinking back to my days as a staff writer on *Welcome Back, Kotter,* I recalled one writer-producer whose joke-writing ability really dazzled and intimidated me and whom I desperately wanted to impress. And though my joke didn't make it past the first rewrite (it didn't belong in the scene and was a good cut), this guy had found it hilarious. He even mentioned to me the next day how much he'd liked it, and how sorry he was we'd had to cut it.

Now, as I reflect back with some embarrassment on all those times I tried to slip that joke into some poor script in which it didn't belong, I think I understand more about that joke's staying power with me. After all, it had made one of my joke-writing idols laugh; it had represented my entry into that august company of writers I admired; it had evidently proven, at some level below my conscious awareness, that I was funny. No wonder I'd been so faithful to it in return. I *owed* it, big time.

Maybe you can remember that the next time you're having a tough time killing a precious darling. Don't be too hard on it, or on yourself. And when you do finally have to kill it—and you probably will—make it as painless as possible. Some part of yourself, small though significant, may be going with it.

Writing Begets Writing

So far, we've talked about (among other things) writer's block, the buddy system, and the sad fact about killing your precious darlings. All of which, however, are subsumed under what I modestly consider the One and Only Cosmic Truth of the writer's life.

It's a maxim I repeat to my clients so often that it's in danger of becoming a mantra—or, at the very least, a bumper sticker. Not exactly earth shaking, or even that original, it goes like this: Writing begets writing.

Simple enough, and I think quite able to stand up under rigorous examination. Regardless of the issues a writer struggles with—creative blocks, procrastination, fear of failure, etc.—the very act of writing tends to stoke the energy, continue the flow, direct the current of further writing.

Writing begets writing. If you're stuck on a difficult scene, write it anyway. Write it badly, obviously, burdened with cliches. Write it in verse.

If you're frustrated at being stuck, or angry at yourself

for your artistic limitations, write about *that*, as a journal entry, pure stream of consciousness. Write out your obsessive, self-shaming thoughts as a Dennis Miller–inspired rant. But write about them.

Or, if you're in a productive mood, give those angry, self-critical feelings to a character in your script or story. If there isn't a likely candidate, invent one. There *is* one, anyway: you. Your anguish and doubt, fears and frustrations, are as elemental and vital to what you're writing as any character or plot point. Might as well make use of this fact.

Writing begets writing. Just as worrying begets more worrying. Obsessing begets more obsessing. Pacing back and forth begets more—

Well, you get the idea.

When you risk writing from where you're at, you set in motion a whole set of internal processes. The first rotten sentence you write has a life you can inhabit, evaluate, cross out. To be replaced by a second, hopefully less rotten sentence. Maybe a good piece of description, a nice turn of phrase, a sharp line of dialogue.

Then again, maybe not. But it doesn't matter. Just keep going. Write the scene, let the characters talk to each other. As novelist and screenwriter William Goldman reminds us, some scenes you write are just "sludge." But they're important connective tissue. They keep things moving. Links in a chain. Weak links, perhaps, but you can always go back and strengthen them later.

With what? The knowledge that you've written, for one thing. Because writing doesn't just beget writing. It also begets—and reinforces—the reality that you *can* write. That pages will accumulate.

Carl Jung said, "Neurotics are people who refuse to suffer." He was referring to people who respond to life's painful events by obsessively reliving them, or blaming themselves for not preventing them, or wishing to be someone to whom such things didn't happen—all to avoid truly experiencing the grief, disappointment, and sense of loss that such events evoke.

From the writer's standpoint, "refusing to suffer" means that relentless worrying and obsessing, however painful, are experienced as potentially less painful than what might result from actually *doing* . . . that is, writing. (In other words, excessive ruminating isn't just a type of procrastination. It's actually a form of self-protection.)

Is it painful to write badly? Hell, yes. Is it more painful *not* to write, and leave yourself open to shaming, self-critical meanings that you have to carry around every day? I think it is. Because any writing that gets done, good or bad, means you're on the path, struggling with your material, on the job, being a writer.

Harold Clurman, the famed theater director, was asked once if he lamented the number of bad plays on Broadway. He said, "No, bad work is the manure from which good work emerges."

Believe me, we've all written manure. But, as Clurman suggests, that's okay. It prepares the ground, nourishes the soil. It's part of the writer's foundation, the layers of experience and craft, like strata in the earth. To push the metaphor to the limit, bad writing—like manure—is as inevitable as the sun and the rain, and just as important for growth.

Every hour you spend writing is an hour not spent fretting about your writing. Every day you produce pages is a day you didn't spend sitting at a coffee shop, bitching about not producing any pages.

So pick your favorite quote. Jung or Clurman. Analyst or artist. It all comes down to the same thing.

Writing begets writing.

Not writing begets . . . well, *not* writing.

You do the math.

Part Two

YOU ARE ENOUGH

*When the last dime is gone, I'll sit out on the
curb with a pencil and a ten-cent notebook,
and start the whole thing all over again.*

— PRESTON STURGES

It's a growth industry—the hundreds of books, tapes, and videos available on the craft of writing; the multitudes of conferences, seminars, and workshops (some of which I've taught myself over the years); the teachers and coaches and gurus promising to reveal the secrets of the "can't-miss" premise, the "never-fails" plot structure, the "you-can't-help-but-love-'em" lead characters.

But in the cacophony of instruction and inspiration competing for the writer's ear, it seems to me a quote from Ray Bradbury emerges from the din. "There is only one type of story in the world—*your* story."

In all the writing classes I've ever taught, that was always the first quote I put on the blackboard. And now, as a therapist, the essence of that quote is what underlies my support for clients struggling to write out of the depths of their own particular truths, no matter how painful or contradictory.

41

I recall an incident, years ago, when I was screenwriter-in-residence at San Francisco State University. I was working with a group of young writers-to-be, one of whom had just read a scene from his script, a political thriller, to the rest of the class. Unfortunately, the scene—in which the hero is trapped by bad guys in a dingy back alley—was flat and uninvolving, though the writer clearly had talent. Moreover, the writing itself seemed tentative, careful.

I asked the writer what would happen if, instead of his hero, he himself were the guy trapped in that alley.

"You mean, if that were *me*?" He suddenly became quite animated, as he described the sequence of scary, funny incidents that would befall him. A scene emerged that was unique, and particular to a very specific sort of individual—a guy like himself. A human being.

"But this guy's gotta be a hero," he said afterward. "Like in the movies."

"He is," I replied. "*Your* hero."

The problem with this student's scene was his attempt to portray what a hero should be like. The writing seemed tentative as a result of the tension within him caused by the effort to exclude his own feelings, doubts, and impulses, as though they were inappropriate for a movie hero.

The irony—and the point of Bradbury's quote—is that *all writing is autobiographical.* Even the student's attempt to write a hero "like in the movies" revealed an aspect of his autobiography; namely, his belief about how a hero needed to behave.

Like it or not, our writing reveals who we are.

The story doesn't matter. The genre doesn't matter. Even if you're writing a historical novel about Sir Francis Drake, your autobiography informs that story: your own attitude toward heroics, what sources you choose to research, vague memories of some pirate movie you saw as a kid, your fantasies about the "freedom of the seas" or whatever. Even your concern about whether or not your novel will be commercial is part of your experience writing it.

On the plus side, it's one of the paradoxes of writing that the more particular and personal a detail in character or story, the more powerfully its impact generalizes out to the audience. (The specifics of Rocky Balboa's life in the first *Rocky* film were shared by few in the audience, I'm sure, but everyone understood what he meant by "going the distance.")

I repeat: All writing is autobiographical. The more you can accept and acknowledge this, the greater the extent to which you can mine your own feelings and experiences to give shape and texture to your work.

Of course, to write from this place, the core of who we are, is damned hard. Often the results are just painful, ambiguous, unformed. *Maybe there's something wrong with me*, the writer thinks. *Maybe I'm not enough.*

That's why writing seminars and workshops flourish; why how-to books on writing are perennial sellers. Intentionally or not, they validate our belief in some key or technique that ensures success; something outside of ourselves that we need to learn or to become.

And, yes, every writer needs to learn story construction, needs to develop craft. But the most important thing a writer needs is the awareness that he or she is enough. That one's feelings, enthusiasms, regrets, hopes, doubts, yearnings, loves, and hates are, in fact, the raw materials of one's writing talent.

"There is only one type of story in the world—*your*

43

story." Which means only *you* can tell it, no matter what form—thriller, romantic comedy, sci-fi adventure—it takes.

This reminds me of another quote I like, from Ralph Waldo Emerson, a pretty fair writer himself. He said, "To believe that what is true for you in your private heart is true for all men—*that* is genius."

Simple, but Not Easy

Now I want to talk about the most important thing a writer must know how to do—which, for lack of a better phrase, is just to *get out of his or her own way.* Or as cellist Pablo Casals said about playing music well, "Learn the notes and forget about 'em."

Simple, isn't it? You have a story to tell, plot beats to tell it, characters to live it, and the will to write it. (You may even have a deal to deliver it.) All you have to do is get out of the way and let the writing happen.

Like I said, simple, right? Hmmm . . .

As a former teacher of mine once remarked, "It may be simple, but it ain't easy."

For years, as a writer, I struggled to get out of my own way, without really understanding what that meant. The phrase always had a kind of down-home, common-sense, don't-make-such-a-big-deal-out-of-it quality that made me frustrated with myself for my difficulty in achieving it. (Similar to my response to the advice to just "be myself"

45

whenever I was anxious about some upcoming interpersonal conflict. Again, simple but not easy.)

As it's generally understood, getting out of your own way implies somehow putting aside the anxieties and doubts, ego concerns and career pressures, mental blocks and critical inner voices—pick your favorite pet term—that stand between you and the effortless flow of writing. As though, if you just did enough therapy, or meditated enough, or manifested enough positive energy, you could disavow all the "stuff" that gets in the way of your creativity.

If only, in other words, you were different from who you are.

Because the simple fact is, we *do* bring our "stuff" to the writing, stuff that runs the gamut from the ridiculous to the sublime, the irritating to the overwhelming. Some writers can't get past their fear of failure; some struggle with a nagging sense of inadequacy regarding their talent; some feel the pressure of being unknown and thus feeling powerless (or even, ironically, the reverse: Norman Mailer once talked of the feeling of creative paralysis that came over him after he'd achieved fame. "It wasn't just *me* sitting down to write," he said. "It was *Norman Mailer* sitting down to write. I had to live up to *him*.")

Add to that the relationship issues, financial pressures, marketplace fluctuations, and sense of isolation that writers must contend with on a daily basis—and suddenly the amount of stuff you're supposed to put aside in order to get out of your own way starts to feel like a veritable mountain of personal baggage.

That's because it *is*. Each of us lugs around enough baggage to warrant the name *Samsonite*. It's the trait we share with every other human being. Our stuff is who we are. Our hopes and fears, loves and hatreds, fantasies and habits and prejudices and favorite movies and the way we tie our shoes and whether we like asparagus and on and on and on. That's us. Human beings.

One particular subset of human beings, those who write, have all the same stuff as the rest of the tribe, except for the need and desire to write about it. We may call what writers write stories, or scripts, or novels, poems, or songs. But what writers really do is write about their stuff, in a language or medium or form that makes what they write understandable to others. In other words, stuff talking to stuff.

Now comes the paradox. If I, the writer, get out of my own way—that is, put my stuff aside so I can write—what's left to write about? My stuff is the raw material of my writing.

In fact, I'll go out on a limb and just say it: There is nothing *but* stuff. Which is great, because that means I'll never run out of raw material. As long as I'm a human being, I have an inexhaustible supply.

Wait a minute. I began by stating that the most important thing a writer had to do was get out of his or her own way. Haven't I just challenged this statement? No. I'm challenging the conventional view of what that means. From my perspective, a writer who invites *all* of who he or she is into the mix—who sits down to work engulfed in stuff, yet doesn't give these thoughts and feelings a negative connotation; who in fact strives to accept and integrate whatever thoughts and feelings emerge—*this* writer has truly gotten out of his or her own way.

From this standpoint, only by labeling a thought or feeling as either good or bad, productive or harmful, are you potentially getting in your own way, restricting your creative flow.

47

Getting out of your own way means being *with* who you are, moment to moment, whether you like it or not. And then being with your liking or not liking it, and writing from that place.

Whew! As I said, simple but not easy.

What Really Happened. . . .

As you know by now, I believe all writing is autobiographical. No matter how seemingly removed in time and space from the reality of your own life, you're writing about yourself. Even your impulse to tell a particular story arises from an aspect of your interior world.

That said, I want to recount an interesting session with a writer client whose short story was getting repeatedly rejected. The story was based on a powerful event from her childhood, one that we'd explored often in therapy—which had in part prompted her to use it as the basis for a work of fiction.

She sat now in my office, depressed and bewildered. "I don't understand it. The last two editors I sent it to said they loved the writing, and the story. But they *hated* the ending."

"Maybe you need to look at it again. Rethink it."

"You mean, *change* it?" She looked up at me, confused. "But I can't. It's what really happened."

Her response reminded me of the classes I'd taught years before on turning autobiography into screenplays. Often, students would mine incidents from their own lives and turn them into narratives that failed to provide a satisfactory resolution to the story. No matter how compelling the autobiographical source material, the story didn't work as a story. To which the student invariably replied, "But that's the way it really happened."

"No," I was always tempted to say, "that's your *experience* of what happened."

There is no objective truth in any event, insofar as the meanings we derive from it. The event is always remembered through the filter of our particular feelings, prejudices, and needs. Every memory serves, however unconsciously, our own agenda. The truth in autobiographical writing resides in the self-experience of the writer, not in any objective rendering of the events. (As someone once said, reading Freud doesn't teach you about man; it teaches you about Freud.)

So, in terms of fiction based on personal experience, to be slavishly devoted to the truth is impossible, on the one hand, and may be detrimental to the narrative, on the other.

Yes, all writing is autobiographical. *And* a creation, an imaginative act. The moment an incident from your own life is conceptualized as having possibilities as a story or script, *the incident begins to change*. Let's imagine an incident: say, the time your Aunt Betty, making cookies in the kitchen, cried at the sudden news of her son's death, but kept making the cookies, hands shaking as she kneaded the dough, because they had been his favorite.

Now, as the impulse to use this incident for a story arises, something happens. Your imagination and craft—even your desire to use the incident—renders it no longer merely a memory from your past, but a story to be shaped. Events are changed, truncated, altered in sequence; people—or, as they should now be called, "characters"—are combined for clarity's sake, or even eliminated. Emphasis is shifted, so that the incident's narrative forms a cohesive whole, with a set-up that builds with mounting intensity to a (hopefully) powerful ending.

In other words, what started as a poignant moment from your childhood has become a scene in your novel or screenplay, and therefore fodder for the sometimes ruthless demands of aesthetic and craft. Cookies too cute?—make it something else. Why not needlepoint, which would get Betty out of the kitchen (which is good, because you already used the kitchen for the big divorce argument scene). Besides, if Betty's in the living room, Mom can be present. Hell, if Mom's there, the news of the son's death doesn't have to come by phone. *She* could tell Betty—Jesus, what's *that* like, having to deliver such awful news? Hmmm . . . maybe this is really *Mom's* scene, not Betty's.

And so it goes. Memory becomes scene, grist for the creative mill. And yet no less meaningful for the writer, regardless of the permutations, because the original spark, the artistic impulse that latched onto that memory and saw its potential, came out of authentic feeling. The story's ultimate form is irrelevant to the process of mining autobiographical material for fiction.

As my client struggled with the idea that narrative concerns might demand that events in her memory be altered or reshaped, she realized she felt a profound need to be loyal to what really happened. It took her a while to reconcile the demands of storytelling versus the requirements of loyalty to her personal history, to the people in her life whose stories she was, after all, appropriating for her own ends.

Which is, as I told her, what writers do.

Case in point: I was only three years old in 1954, and I grew up in an Italian household in Pittsburgh, not a Jewish one in New York, but that family in *My Favorite Year* was my family.

Was and wasn't. That's what writers do.

"For I Have Done Good Work"

At the end of part one, I presented a belief of mine that underlies much of my work with writer clients; namely, that writing begets writing. As a corollary to this belief, I also feel strongly that the work itself—the practice of the craft of writing—must be its own reward.

I'm not referring here to some sort of abstract, intellectual ideal. When I say the work should be its own reward, I mean that in the most concrete, pragmatic way. The rewards, while often private and intensely subjective, are nonetheless real: the satisfaction of artistic growth; the realization of one's vision; the engagement with one's interior world, and the creative expansiveness enjoyed by communicating this world to others.

In short, happiness.

The preceding definition of happiness might strike some as unusual, but it makes perfect sense to me. Robert Louis Stevenson once wrote, "I know what happiness is, for I have done good work."

Admittedly, this can be a tough concept to grasp in a marketplace obsessed with financial success. We tend to judge a work—novel, film, TV show—successful in terms of its "numbers," not its intrinsic qualities, nor even the level of satisfaction and enjoyment it supplies its readers or audience. For me to suggest that you—or anyone, for that matter—should think about a creative work based on the subjective experience of joy the writer derived from *doing* it seems, well . . . nuts.

And that's okay with me. We live in the real world, after all. Marketplace concerns are valid and irrefutable. Their impact on the life of a writer is tangible and important. Just ask a screenwriter who's been in script development for over a year and has just been replaced by another writer. Just ask a TV writer who's been sweating out a particularly brutal hiring season, only to end up unemployed. Just ask the novelist whose publisher has cut back on its proposed book list, nullifying author contracts and asking that advances be returned.

It's neither possible nor desirable to transcend the demands of the real world. But the writer's life has its own set of demands, equally valid and important, that must also be attended to. In fact, if they are ignored, "good work," as Stevenson referred to it, rarely emerges anyway, so there's no product to sell to the marketplace.

What does a writer's life demand, or require? To my mind, the most important requirement is the true, personal engagement with the work itself, the sheer love of the practice of one's craft.

When asked the secret of contentment, a Hindu sage replied, "Absorption." For a writer, I believe, the secret of contentment lies similarly in absorption in the work, in fully

54

inhabiting that secret place co-created by you and that which is being written. In so believing in the reality of the world of your book or script that what happens in the narrative seems as inevitable as the sunrise, and that how the characters act seems to emerge from their own inherent truthfulness. The work *flows,* to borrow a term from author and researcher Milhaly Csikszentmihalyi, as though it has a life of its own.

Which, of course, it does. A life you've given it. And that's the point. When I watch my novelist clients struggling with the reality of their publisher's indifference, or share my screenwriter clients' fears about what seems to be a shrinking feature film market, I'm always struck by the sobering fact that writers rarely have a sense of their own power. The "life" that writers give to story and character—that, in fact, they provide the fields of publishing and entertainment in their entirety—comes solely from the power residing within the writer to challenge himself or herself creatively, to explore his or her own subjective world of experience and imagination. This is as much a gift as it is a talent, and if writers themselves don't respect it, who will?

As writing begets writing, so does good work, I believe, beget happiness. Certainly, if happiness is defined as emerging from an authentic connection with oneself and one's work, between oneself and one's purpose. For writers today, to be true to such an ideal places them at the end of a long line of artists, a literal "chain of being," that stretches back to the first artists. This is a tradition that honors writers as truth-seekers, explicators of the wealth of human feelings, chroniclers of our aspirations and failures. As such, this makes writers (and the lives they lead) difficult, contrary, even dangerous. And frequently unemployable, out of fashion, the wrong sex or color, or just plain "not what we're look-ing for."

Marketplace requirements change with the seasons. Fads come and go. But good work, from which writers have for centuries drawn sustenance and power, is a private matter, a kind of "secret of happiness" residing solely in the artist's heart.

And it's yours to discover, if you choose to, every time you write.

On the Couch

Every once in a while, a writer client will come into my office and announce, "Well, I heard the other day on the radio that we're all crazy."

"Who's crazy?" I ask.

"*Us*. Writers. Artists in general. This shrink was on some talk show on NPR, and he said it's been proven that we're all manic depressives."

"I'm confused. Do you mean that because you're an artist you're manic depressive, or does being manic depressive cause you to be an artist?"

"He said it could be one or the other, but it could be both. What do you think?"

"I think I'm gonna skip the next NPR pledge drive."

Apparently, it's in fashion again—the notion that the creative impulse, with its accompanying emotional difficulties, is merely the product of a psychological disorder. The current favorite diagnosis for artists, particularly writers, is bipolar disorder—a condition that used to be called manic depression.

The most recent book to make this argument was the influential *Touched By Fire,* by Kay Jamison. But the idea that writers are of a single and highly neurotic personality type goes all the way back to—who else?—Freud. In the 1950s, a fellow named Edmund Bergler (credited, by the way, with inventing the term *writer's block*) wrote many books on the subject. His explanation for the reason that writers write? "Psychic masochism."

(My friend Al Hutter, a psychoanalyst, not only objects to Bergler's theories, but laments how often he got them into print. As Al puts it, "Unfortunately, the only person who writes about the term 'writer's block' but appears never to have suffered from it is Dr. Edmund Bergler.")

Obviously, the idea that the artistic impulse is inevitably the product of a psychological condition is not new. After all, history is filled with examples of the tormented artist stricken by melancholy, going on drunken binges, cutting off an ear, and generally behaving—as we therapists like to say—inappropriately. But to infer that some kind of "craziness" underlies creative endeavor, or, even worse, that the impulse to create is itself an indicator of some condition is just plain wrong.

First, to whatever extent a therapist believes in the validity of diagnostic labels like "bipolar," one thing is clear: Labels exist for the convenience of the labeler. How helpful they are to the artistic person is debatable.

(I recall a radio interview with a family therapist who claimed that 98 percent of Americans were co-dependent—I found this as helpful as saying that 98 percent of Americans walk around on two feet. Ascribing a label to an entire group renders the label superfluous.)

Second, claiming that the creative impulse comes from any one source—whether mania, psychosis, or the moon—is both ludicrous and potentially harmful. Ludicrous because it's oversimplified and inconsistent with the lived experience of countless artists. Potentially harmful because it undervalues the mysterious, indefinable aspects of the creative act.

I'm reminded of a quote by H. L. Mencken, who said, "There is always an easy solution to every human problem—neat, plausible, and wrong." The tendency to see a writer's emotional (or even creative) struggles solely in terms of their being a problem—and thus potentially solvable—betrays a profound narrowness in scope, imagination, and appreciation for the hidden ways of the artistic heart.

A similar narrowness of vision underlies the current fervor for defining the creative person in pathological ways and seeing his or her artistic struggles not as the manifestation of the chaos from which creativity emerges but as symptoms of a particular neurotic type.

The point is, yes, perhaps Van Gogh *did* suffer from symptoms that we might label manic depressive. But what is also true—and certainly more important—is that he was incredibly talented. Both facts can coexist, without one necessarily causing the other.

As always, I'm struck by our desire to take that which defies explanation and try to reduce it to some kind of rational terms. Whether residing in the rules of all the how-to books on writing currently in print, or emerging from the latest analytic theories, or championed in studies from the academic community, we seem to need to make sense of creativity, to isolate its source in some concrete way.

And we always fail. Its magic continues to elude us. Thank God.

The novelist John Fowles put it best: "For what good science tries to eliminate, good art seeks to provoke—*mystery*, which is lethal to the one, and vital to the other."

"You're No John Updike!"

Finally, let's talk about the major obstacle to sustaining a belief that you are enough: namely, comparing yourself to other writers.

Not a week goes by in my practice that I don't hear a client sing the praises of some work he or she has just read, accompanied by the following lament: "I'll *never* write anything that good! I'm not talented enough [or smart enough, funny enough, deep enough, etc.]. I mean, who am I kidding?"

I remember one client in particular, who was hard at work on a movie thriller, comparing his script unfavorably to *Chinatown*. "Let's face it," he said. "I'm no Robert Towne."

It reminded me of the vice-presidential debate a dozen years ago in which Dan Quayle, in defense of his perceived inexperience, compared his qualifications for high office with those of John F. Kennedy. To which his opponent, Lloyd Bentsen, famously rebutted, "I knew Jack Kennedy, and you, sir, are no Jack Kennedy!"

Fairly or not, Bentsen struck a nerve, because comparisons are one of the primary ways in which we evaluate and discern. It certainly echoes the horrible comparisons to others that most of us endured as children in our families, or at school. We live in a competitive culture, after all, and thus we soon join our parents, teachers, and society at large in comparing ourselves to our peers, our rivals, our leaders, the famous.

Writers are as competitive as any other group, if not more so. In fact, in my experience, the only thing that changes over time is the name of the person the writer is comparing himself to. For years, it was Robert Towne or Neil Simon or Stephen King. John Grisham's name has come up a lot in my office, particularly the year he was also named one of *People* magazine's "Fifty Most Beautiful People." Clients have routinely tormented themselves over the talents (and careers) of such diverse writers as Joyce Carol Oates, David Mamet, the two Annes (Tyler and Rice), John Le Carre, and Sue Grafton.

As of this writing, the specter of TV writer David E. Kelley comes up most often among clients seeking to make themselves miserable, and for three very good reasons: He's a fast writer, he's a successful writer (the creator of *Ally McBeal, The Practice,* and *Chicago Hope,* among others), *and* he's married to Michelle Pfeiffer.

In my view, comparing your career with that of some well-known, accomplished writer is a waste of time, not only because it adds to the shameful self-recrimination most struggling writers already endure, but because it misses the point.

When my client, the guy writing the mystery script, said, "I'm no Robert Towne," my first response was to agree with him. And then to go on from there to what his concerns were really about.

The reality is, every writer *can't* be Robert Towne, or John Updike or Preston Sturges or Ernest Hemingway or Jane Austen. For one thing, those writers beat you to it. *They're* them. That job's been filled.

More important, they're not the writers you're really in competition with. No matter how successful you are, no matter your level of talent, your true competition is yourself.

Think of it this way: Maybe every writer can't be Proust, but every writer can be a better writer. Comparing yourself to others not only deflates and devalues your own efforts, but actually mitigates against the very thing that has the potential to improve your writing—the private connection to your inner world of experience, that wellspring of authentic feeling and desire from which the impulse to write arises.

When I say that your true competition is yourself, I'm referring to your willingness to engage daily with what's going on inside you, your courage to dig deeper, your passion to know what it is you really think and feel and to find creative expression for it.

I'll go a step further. I would argue that, painful as it seems, it's actually easier to endure feelings of inferiority than to challenge yourself to grow as an artist. In fact, in my own life, when I'm tempted to devalue my work in comparison to others', I've learned to see it as a red flag, a kind of warning beacon alerting me to look back at myself and see where I might feel stuck, unmotivated, uninspired. Invariably, if I explore my working process honestly, I'll find that comparing myself to others was triggered by a lack of excitement or commitment to what I was working on.

Yes, we live in the real world, a world of competition and yearning and loss, where on bad days the temptation to compare yourself to others is almost irresistible. But if you really look at what you're doing—hopefully, with compassion as well as insight—you'll see that your only competition, your true challenge, is to be who you are, and to write from that place.

Which means, okay, maybe you're no John Updike. But when you're writing from a place of excitement and authentic feeling, who needs to be?

Part Three

GRIST FOR THE MILL

All serious daring starts from within.
— EUDORA WELTY

Feelings are information. Writers, like all craftspeople, depend on information to further their work. At the end of the last chapter, I talked about the danger of comparing your work with that of other writers. But what about the feelings underlying such comparisons? Feelings like envy, doubt, and fear?

In my view, such emotional colors are as much a part of a writer's palette as his or her ideas, dreams, and memories. Whether referred to as raw materials, the stuff of life, or grist for the mill, the meaning's the same. We inhabit and co-create with others a world of feelings, painful and pleasant, exhilarating and depleting. Every important detail of our lives is dotted with emotional reference points, layered with attitudes and prejudices, shadowed by joy or regret.

In a word, information. To the extent to which a writer can access this information, and own it, this is the degree to which his or her work compels the reader to keep reading— to continue exploring, in tandem with the writer, the commonality of their experience as fellow human beings.

Envy

We might as well start here, with envy. I'm thinking about a screenwriter client I saw recently. Despite some of the gains he'd made in therapy, he felt his work was continually undermined by his envy of other writers.

He'd had to stop reading the Hollywood trade papers, he told me, because seeing the deals being made by others angered and deflated him. He'd grown increasingly self-critical about his work habits—normally a source of pride and satisfaction—since hearing rumors about a well-known screenwriter's penchant for "knocking out a script" in a week. It had reached a point where learning of a friend's having lunch with a studio executive or potential new agent could trigger a depression.

None of these feelings were unfamiliar to me. During my own screenwriting career, it almost seemed as though envy was the ocean my friends and I swam in, including my friends who wrote novels or poetry, or did magazine work.

To me, envy was the dirty little secret of the writing life. Except it was the worst-kept secret I'd ever known.

For some, of course, hearing of another's success was a spur to greater efforts. For others, the result was often a crippling paralysis.

It took me a long time to understand, and to accept, that envy is a natural by-product of the achieving life. Throughout our childhood experiences in our families, and then our schools, and ultimately in the adult world, we strive to achieve in a matrix of others who strive to achieve—such that comparison is not only inevitable, but often the only standard by which to measure that achievement.

With time and maturity, we hopefully develop the self-awareness (and self-acceptance) to measure ourselves by more internal monitors; to enjoy the expression of our creative talents for their own sake.

But we also live in the real world and need the validation of that world. For a writer in a commercial marketplace, that means enduring intense competition and the almost daily spectacle of others enjoying extravagant rewards in fame and money, all while negotiating the often gut-wrenching peaks and valleys of one's own career.

In other words, that means living with envy.

The key to surviving envy, as with all feelings evoked in the stress of the achieving life, is to acknowledge it. By that, I'm not referring merely to the *fact* that you're envious, but also the *meaning* that you give to it.

If a writer sees envy as a sign of some kind of moral weakness or character failing—a view often engendered and reinforced in childhood—the effect on his or her work can be quite debilitating.

Equally harmful is seeing one's envy as a disparaging

Envy

comment on one's work. I once had a client try to disavow her envy of another's success, lest she experience it as confirmation of a lack of faith in her own writing. "If I let myself feel envy," she said, "it means I don't believe in the possibility of my own success."

Another client bravely insisted that "envy is counterproductive." So terrified of anything that might derail his firmly held belief in "positive thinking," the meaning he gave to envy—as well as any other "negative" emotion—was of an insidious obstacle on the tracks of his forward momentum.

Only by investigating what envy means to us can we risk acknowledging it. It's just a feeling, like other feelings—which means it's also information, as I said previously. If nothing else, envy informs us of how important our goals are. It reminds us of the reasons we undertook the creative life in the first place, and challenges us to commit once again to its rigors and rewards.

So the choice is yours. You can deny your envy, or celebrate it. You can talk it to death among your friends, or suffer in silence. Or, hopefully, you can accept it with humor and self-acknowledgment, and perhaps explore what its meaning is for you.

But one thing I know. For a writer, to coin a phrase, nothing's certain except death and taxes. *And* envy.

Faith and Doubt

A misspent childhood watching Saturday morning cartoons has left an image indelibly imprinted on my memory, that of a character torn by indecision—a conflict between doing right or wrong—being prodded by a tiny angel whispering in one ear, an equally tiny devil whispering in the other.

Since these stories were aimed at kids, the ethical dilemmas were usually pretty clear-cut, such as whether or not to tie an oversized napkin around your neck and eat your co-star. However, there was still an almost theological impact to seeing funny talking animals—rabbits, ducks, and "puddy cats"—with competing imps sitting on their shoulders, caught in some Warner Brothers version of angst.

This image occurred to me again recently, when I came upon something written by Lillian Smith. "Faith and doubt, both are needed, not as antagonists but working side by side, to take us around the unknown curve."

Often, working with writers, it almost seems as though little twin entities—one named Faith, the other Doubt—sit on *their* shoulders, whispering their respective messages, like those winged imps in the cartoons.

The animated image of these imps is of two competing forces, of which one must inevitably win out. And, of course, one is represented as unequivocally better than the other.

With writers, it's frequently the same. We all want faith to win out over doubt. We want faith whispering constantly in our ear—inspiring us, encouraging us, instilling hope. And make no mistake, these are blandishments every writer needs; it's too daunting a task otherwise.

The mistake, I think, is to strive to banish doubt, to see it as the enemy. Just as courage has no meaning without fear, faith has no meaning without doubt. They're the yin and yang of all aspiration.

As writers, we naturally long to sequester our doubts and fears, to disavow pain and worry. Unfortunately, to vanquish doubt is to leave the domain of the human being. Conversely, to embrace both one's doubt and faith, one's fear and courage, is to relate to the totality of the human experience.

The paradox of struggling with doubt—as with all so-called negative feelings—is that only by inviting it in, exploring and illuminating its meanings, can we be enriched as writers. The plain fact is, the more willing you are to mine the landscape of your own doubts, the truer and more recognizably human your characters will be. (And the more impact your characters' faith, if such is their destination, will have.)

Keeping the tension between faith and doubt alive within you, without either falling prey to blind optimism or succumbing to despair, is not easy. We veer so often in one direction or the other that, in their exaggerated forms, faith and doubt can look like two sides of the same coin.

"But how can that be?" you might be asking. Faith and doubt are so different, such opposites. Not necessarily, not when taken to extremes.

Let me give you an example. Picture two clients, both struggling writers. One is full of confidence, with the faith of a saint in the ultimate success of his career goals. He feels great about everything he writes. All he has to do is wait for the literary world to discover him.

The second client is full of doubt. He took a writing class at a local junior college, but quit after just two meetings. He won't show his work to others because "they'll probably hate it." He's just wasting his time trying to write, because the odds against success are so huge.

Faith and doubt, two sides of the same coin. Whether a writer subscribes to one or the other, he or she is engaged in a kind of "magical thinking" that leaves him or her out of the equation. In writing, as in all aspects of life, an unquestioning faith is the same as unwavering doubt—both are belief systems employed to try to protect a person from the complicated, sometimes contradictory, always unpredictable ebb and flow of actual experience.

"Faith and doubt, both are needed. . . ."

Which brings us back to those Saturday morning cartoons. The truth is, if we each had imps named Faith and Doubt parked on our shoulders, competing for airtime, the ideal situation would be for their voices to stay at more or less equal volume, for our attention to shift from one to the other, and back again.

And, ultimately, for us to integrate what each has to say, and to struggle to create and thrive from that place within us where *all* feelings—including faith and doubt—reside.

Fear

I'd like to say a few words on behalf of fear.

This is probably not going to be a popular position. Among my writer clients, and certainly in the culture at large, fear tops the list of the so-called negative emotions. ("I have no respect for fear," I was once told by a TV producer. "Never let 'em see you sweat," urged a well-known deodorant commercial.)

However, if you've read this far, you know that I believe feelings are neither good nor bad; they just *are,* and the more access we have to them, the more authentic we are in the world. And the more truth, power, and relevance our writing has.

Which sounds good only in the abstract, I admit. Because for a writer paralyzed by fear—whether in midsentence, midmeeting, or midcareer—the feelings of anxiety, danger, and potential shaming self-recrimination are very concrete. Who wouldn't want to banish fear?

I certainly did, many years ago, when research for a screenplay led to my attempting a climb of the Grand Teton, a mountain peak in Wyoming. Though at this particular moment, I wasn't exactly climbing. I was sitting on a ledge, a good thousand feet below the summit, shaking.

Andy, my climbing instructor, asked me what was going on.

"I'm afraid," I said, glancing up at the forbidding rockface.

"Good," he replied. "Otherwise, I wouldn't climb with you."

He went on to tell me about his own fears, which were still with him after climbing all over the world, including four trips to Everest.

"Fear keeps you in the here-and-now," he explained. "Which keeps you alive up here. So stay in touch with it—and just keep slogging up the mountain."

As it turned out, staying in touch with my fear wasn't the problem. It was staying in touch with anything *else*—everything I'd learned, practiced, rehearsed in my mind a dozen times the night before the climb.

Then, as I found the next hand- or foot-hold, or made the next traverse, I slowly began to understand what Andy had been talking about. The fear became a part of how I was taking in each moment; a feeling in a mosaic of feelings. Not something to be pushed away, or willed out of existence, but a kind of electrical current running through the circuits of my experience.

The fear was a prod, a warning, a partner in each split second of decision making. It stopped my breath, which reminded me to breathe again. It tensed my muscles, which reminded me to relax them. At 15,000 feet, with yawning emptiness falling away below me, it focused my attention—and then some—on the inch-wide crack in the rockface, just wide enough for curved gloved fingers to jam in.

By the time I'd reached the summit, aching and exhausted, the exultation I felt, the shout of triumph that escaped my lips, was as much an honoring of the fear that had accompanied me up the mountain as it was the relief of surviving it.

Which brings me back to that producer who said he had no respect for fear. He might as well have said, "I have no respect for an integral part of myself." Like most of us, he was giving a negative meaning to his fear—that it was a sign of weakness, some shadow part of himself that, if acknowledged, would say something damaging about him.

But every healthy person has fear and uses it to navigate in the world, to assess situations and avoid danger. Even so-called imaginary fears—like the belief that you'll die if your novel is rejected—are signals of potential danger, of painful consequences to be avoided. As we explore and understand the meaning we assign these fears, we hopefully learn the tools to coexist with them.

Even more so, as writers, our job is to mine these fears and their particular meanings for us, so that our work becomes vivid and multidimensional, that it hums with life.

If we try to sequester our fears, leave them out of the equation, then much of our creative energy—that "electrical current" I experienced on my climb—is drained away. No fear, then no release from fear. No anxiety, then no anticipatory rush.

It's as though, to scale the mountain of our writing craft, we need excitement and fear to get us to the top.

Which leads me again to that windswept summit of the

Grand Teton, where Andy and I stood those many years ago.
He asked how the climb had gone for me.

"I was half excited, half terrified," I told him.

"Sounds about right," he said.

The Judge

Among the majority of my writer clients, a salient concern is the struggle against one's "inner critic," the persistent, sometimes harsh, and almost always shaming voice that belittles or invalidates one's work. Indeed, the term *inner critic* is such a well-known concept in our culture that millions of dollars are spent on books, tapes, and seminars promising to silence—or even banish—this punishing element of most people's inner world.

The problem with this approach, in my view, is twofold: The goal of killing off the self-critical, judgmental part of your psyche confirms the idea that there's something wrong with you that needs to be fixed; that there's a perfectable "you" in the future who's unencumbered by such conflicts.

Not to mention my second objection, which is that it isn't even possible.

Unquestionably, there's nothing more painful about the writing process than struggling against feelings of self-doubt, even self-loathing. I've worked with clients who literally hate everything they write—it's not good enough, funny enough, commercial enough. Even those with a more balanced view of their output acknowledge the stress of continually having to keep deeply critical inner voices at bay to get through the damn thing.

"Killing off" one's inner critic won't work; it isn't even desirable. It's part of who you are, a necessary part, as much as your enthusiasm, your work habits, your loves and hates, your joys and regrets. Because, like these other aspects of your emotional life, an inner critic is a two-edged sword.

Think of it this way: The same inner critic that judges our work so severely provides us with the ability to discern our likes and dislikes, to form opinions, to make decisions. It reinforces the faith in our subjective experience that allows us to choose *this* rather than *that*.

We need a sense of judgment to navigate in the world. The amount and intensity of that judgment, as with most things, lies along a continuum; hopefully, we possess neither too much nor too little.

Imagine waiting to cross the street at a busy intersection: With too little judgment, you might ignore the "Don't Walk" sign and get run over; with too much judgment, you stand frozen even when the sign reads "Walk," and therefore never get anywhere.

What I'm trying to suggest here is that we don't judge our *having* an inner judge too harshly. Writing in the face of a persistent inner critic is draining enough. To compound the problem by blaming yourself for being engaged in the struggle is ridiculous.

Remember, too, what I said about your inner critic being a two-edged sword. Because if we can accept with self-compassion this troubling aspect of ourselves, we might even learn something.

I'm thinking of an example from my own experience as a client in therapy. This was many years ago, when I was struggling with some very painful issues, specifically a rather profound fear of failure that seemed unaffected by my outward success. The sessions were so gut wrenching, I thought about quitting therapy.

Yet I kept coming, week after week, much to my own surprise. When I mentioned this to my therapist, he suggested that while the issues underlying my fear of failure were indeed painful and difficult, it was this same fear of failure that kept me coming back to therapy every week. In other words, the same thing that was causing the problem was providing the determination to keep slugging away at it. I just wouldn't quit.

That's when I realized what a two-edged sword my particular problem was. Almost every aspect of our emotional life has an affirming and an invalidating component. Our job, then, is to examine an issue that troubles us—a harsh inner critic, for example—and learn what is both positive and negative about it, in terms of our work and our life.

If we approach our inner critic from this perspective, that of a life-long process of examination, we can coexist with it. Along with feeling the pain of its intense scrutiny, we also develop the courage to challenge the self-defeating meanings we give to that pain. This has always been the artist's struggle, what Rollo May calls "the courage to create."

Or, to put it bluntly: You're a writer. Which means, you're your own worst critic. Join the club.

Double-Barreled Blues

There are two elements—two truths, really—of the writer's life that contribute to making it so difficult, frustrating, and, at times, almost surrealistic. Over the years, as both a writer and a therapist, I've witnessed the sometimes numbing, often dispiriting effect of these two truths. It's something I call the double-barreled blues.

The first barrel contains a well-known aphorism (with which people in 12-step programs are certainly familiar), which goes something like this: "The definition of 'crazy' is doing the same thing over and over, without success, in the expectation that it will eventually work."

Well, as every struggling TV and film writer knows, the way to break into the business is by writing spec scripts and networking friends and other possible connections. That's it. Writing and networking. If, however, you've written your spec and exhausted your network of contacts, with disappointing results, the next thing to do is—

Write another spec and keep networking.

If you're trying to break into magazine journalism, you have to write query letters to editors, strap a cell phone to your ear so you don't miss calls from possible sources, and stay current on trends in trade publishing. If, however, you've done these things for a good length of time without getting an assignment, the next thing to do is—

Write more query letters, make more phone calls.

In other words, keep doing the same thing over and over, each time in the hopes that the outcome will be different. This is the very definition, according to the folk wisdom quoted previously, of being crazy.

No wonder writers struggle with depression, fatigue, and feelings of despair. It's how the game is set up. Writing and networking, again and again, until you land an agent, or sell an article, or snag a job on a TV series. And it's the only game in town. Who *wouldn't* feel crazy?

And that's just the first shot of the double-barreled blues. The second is a belief, nurtured since childhood and reinforced in everyday life, in the validity of cause and effect. You know, along the lines of "If you eat your spinach, you'll grow up big and strong." "If you do your homework, you'll get good grades." "If you leap off a cliff, sooner or later you're going to hit the bottom."

In almost every area of life, even factoring in such real variables as luck, family of origin, and where you went to school (and with whom), cause and effect seems to apply. Work hard and things happen. Work harder, and more things happen.

Except when it comes to writing. You'd think that the better your writing becomes, the more likely your chances of success. And it's true. But it's also *not* true.

Bang! There's that second barrel.

Every day my clients complain that their best work goes unsold, while their worst writing is rewarded. Clients who've struggled for years, assuming that talent and hard work should earn them success, grow more and more disheartened. Until, unexpectedly, an agent responds, or an editor buys a story idea.

"Why now?" the client asks. "Why not years ago, or six months ago? Why today, and not yesterday?"

In other words, what exactly was the cause that produced this particular effect? (And, more important, can we bottle it?)

There you have it, the double-barreled blues of a writer's life: first, that the only way to succeed is to keep on keeping on, despite the lack of tangible results; and second, the sobering reality that cause and effect, the underlying force in the rest of the universe, works only intermittently when it comes to writing.

Sounds pretty gloomy, doesn't it? Damn right. That's why sometimes it seems like you need a will of iron, the hide of a rhino, and the hubris of a god to be a writer. And, make no mistake, you *do*.

But you also need something else, something I've mentioned before, throughout this book: namely, you need a relationship with your writing talent that exists apart from the vagaries of your day-to-day struggles. A benign, ongoing, mutually replenishing relationship between yourself and your creativity.

I'm not talking about some grandiose detachment from the painful realities of the writing life. For one thing, I don't believe such transcendence is possible. I don't even think it's desirable. The inner world of a good writer is engaged with everything in his or her subjective experience, which includes struggling with the double-barreled blues (as well as reveling in mastery of craft, enjoying financial success, taking pride in creative achievement, etc.). It's all grist for the mill.

To keep from being ground up in that mill, however, you have to find a way to coexist with the realities of the writer's life. You have to challenge yourself to continue on, integrating both the good and the bad in your experience, being as fluid and open as possible with whatever comes.

Even when it comes at you with both barrels.

Myths, Fairy Tales, and Woody Allen

You know the scene: the opening sequence of Woody Allen's *Stardust Memories*. A glum Woody sits in a dark, dingy train car, with other lost souls. Looking out the window, he sees another train car—shining, brightly lit. Inside, beautiful men and women laugh and drink champagne, a festive vision of wit and privilege out of a Noel Coward play. Woody despairs. Why isn't *he* in the sparkling car, with the sparkling people?

I mention this scene because it comes up almost weekly in my private practice. Among the many myths, metaphors, and fairy tales that inhabit the conscious life of my creative clients, this particular scene emerges again and again.

"I'm doing my life wrong," a client laments. Usually he's just had lunch with a successful producer or big-name publisher who just radiates charm, confidence, and the sense that life is one big party. (With the implication there's a pile of money somewhere in the background to keep the canapés coming.) "I feel like Woody in that train car—the shitty one!" my client says mournfully.

Rivaling this classic scene is another classic—roughly 2500 years old. At least once a month some client compares himself to Sisyphus, the poor guy in Greek mythology condemned to pushing a heavy rock up a steep hill—only to have it come rolling down, at which point his labors begin again. This one's real popular with screenwriters.

The third most mentioned analogy comes from the world of children's fairy tales—the story of the Emperor's new clothes. A vain Emperor, clad only in his underwear, parades in front of his subjects, who've been told to marvel at his new, beautiful garments. Which they all do, until one brave little boy yells out that the Emperor's actually riding around in his longjohns.

This feeling shows up in my office every day. Clients who bristle at some announcement in the news about a much-maligned screenplay getting green-lighted for production, an unlikely new TV show being produced, a *schmaltzy* though wildly successful author signing a multibook deal.

"I *read* that script—it sucks!" the screenwriter client rages. "Why am *I* the only one who sees it?"

"I was *offered* that series," a writer-producer client laughs. "I couldn't turn it down fast enough. It won't last a month."

"*That* putz gets a three-book deal?" a novelist client complains. "How many times can he write the same story? The Emperor's got no clothes, buddy—trust me!"

Aside from their value as metaphors and analogues, these three concepts—the train car, Sisyphus, and the Emperor's new clothes—offer important clues to some of the underlying issues writers often struggle with.

Take the train car: Once, when a sitcom writer used this scene to explain his feelings, what emerged was not only his sense of himself as inadequate, but something else more insidious and undermining. Namely, the idea that he'd been dealt a bad hand—"I'm in the wrong car"—because of *intrinsic defects* in himself. Those happy, glittering people were in the shining train car because they deserved to be there, while he did not. Thereafter, in our work together, his self-sabotaging behaviors could be understood as a natural result of his belief in himself as basically defective. When this painful self-concept was successfully illuminated and challenged, things began to shift in his view of himself.

With another client, a screenwriter who compared himself to Sisyphus, we stayed with this image as a framework to explore issues from within his family. As a child, he'd endured the impossible expectations of his critical, demanding father, a man embittered by business failures. Seeing his own life as valueless, his father placed a great burden on my client to be rich and powerful. One day, during a session, my client blurted out, "Dammit, it's *his* rock I'm pushing up the hill! It's not my rock at all."

"Or maybe even your hill," I offered.

This awareness helped move us in the direction of freeing him from the requirement to fulfill his father's aspirations, and to begin parsing out those goals that were genuinely his.

As for the story of the Emperor's new clothes—well, I think there are two ways of looking at it. Sometimes a writer's own vulnerabilities get the better of him or her. When hearing about another writer's new book deal, for example, authentic feelings of disdain for that person's talent may indeed fuel his or her response. But what may be hidden are painful, unwelcome feelings of shame because his or her *own* career isn't going so well. These shameful feelings are themselves so unacceptable to the writer that he or she covers them over with hearty, frequently sardonic comments about the new book deal—how untalented the author is, how foolish the publisher is, how perpetually gullible the reading public is, and so on.

In psychoanalytic terms, this is often called having a grandiose self-ideal. You liken yourself to the child in the story about the Emperor's clothes because he's seen as the truth-teller, the wisdom figure, the one whose innate intelligence and good sense shatters the illusion. In short, this is just another defense mechanism.

But I believe there's another, more congenial explanation for this story's popularity with writers. It's because writers often *do* assume precisely the role of the kid in the story. Every day, in offices and on conference calls and via e-mail, writers have to fend off, try to interpret, and in a dozen other ways simply deal with the incredible idiocies of their various editors, producers, and agents. Perfectly good TV episodes, for instance, tinkered with by overpaid producers. Logically argued personal essays, reworked by under-achieving journal editors. An exquisitely worked out court-room novel getting an unnecessary sex scene (or two). A searing, erotic screenplay getting *its* sex scenes deleted. And on and on.

The desecration of narrative sense, the elimination of personal style, the dilution of idiosyncratic viewpoint or political outrage that writers have to witness—and usually acquiesce to—simply boggles the mind.

As I will suggest in the next part of this book, the writer is frequently the smartest person in the room. And this is not always so wonderful. Sometimes it's like watching a four-car pile-up unfolding in slow motion—you see everything about to happen; in fact, it seems inevitable—and you're expected not only to shut up about it, but be a willing participant.

So whenever a client compares himself or herself to the kid who points out the truth about the royal wardrobe, it's a short jump to that writer's issues of control, and the painful realization that he or she has in fact very little. The only control a writer has is over himself or herself, the extent to which the writing is done truly and well, and the amount of craft and commitment that's brought to a project. After that, it's up to the gods.

Emperors, Greeks, Woody Allen. The things we make reference to, like the jokes and anecdotes we recount, all have something important to tell us. They deepen our awareness of ourselves as writers and as people. All we have to do is pay attention and do our best.

Which means that, like it or not, at any given moment, we're probably riding the train we're supposed to be on.

The Long View

I saw a full-page ad in a magazine recently that made my jaw drop. It showed a guy wearing some kind of glitzed-up, New Age headphones, smiling blissfully, above copy announcing a breakthrough in consciousness-raising technology. The headline read, "You'll be meditating like a Buddha in thirty minutes!"

In retrospect, I'm surprised I was so surprised. After all, this is the era of the quick fix. Look at our TV ads and infomercials: "Great Abs in Eight Minutes!" "One Month to Financial Security!" "Speak French Like a Frenchman—In One Day!" "Give Us Twenty-Two Minutes, We'll Give You the World!"

Thinking about that magazine ad, it occurred to me that this same kind of quick-fix mentality now pervades the industry that's grown up around writing in recent years. "How to Write a Best-Seller in One Month!" "Write A Movie in Seven Days!" "Create Ten Great Characters Before Lunch!" Books, tapes, and seminars promising a short ride to fame and fortune.

Such fantasies are fueled, too, by the occasional overnight success—the spec screenplay that goes for big money, the best-selling book by some unknown author. What's their secret? we wonder. What tricks do I need to learn?—and *fast!*

To be fair, these workshops can and do offer some valuable craft tips and often provide a much-needed jumpstart for struggling writers. But they miss what I call "the long view."

I'm not talking here about a writer needing patience (which he or she does). Or resilience (another crucial ingredient). I'm not even referring to the steady growth of craft and a deepening commitment to one's authentic voice, which come as a natural by-product of a mature writing process.

I'm referring to something more basic. Strange as it may seem in this era of speed dialing, quick-drying cement, and fast food, I'm suggesting that writers *slow down.*

Let me explain. My problem with the how-to books and seminars that promise instant results is not the array of sure-fire techniques and writing rules they espouse. For one thing, some of these rules are so entrenched as givens now that it would be foolish not to learn them. Besides, there *is* some wisdom in the notion that you have to learn the rules before you can artfully bend them.

No, it's not the techniques I object to, but rather the subtextual message of such approaches: that of supporting a short-term, goal-oriented, "hitting the bull's-eye" kind of life for a writer.

Being a writer—with all its successes and failures, raptures and rejections—is a life-long endeavor. Less a career choice than a calling, its rewards are often so private and ambiguous as to be inexpressible. It's as much a perspective on things, a way of organizing one's experience, as it is a job.

John Fowles opens his novel *Daniel Martin* with this sentence: "Whole sight—or all the rest is desolation." Seeing things whole, having the long view, is the only way to live the writer's life. It's committing yourself to a concept of writing as an integral, ongoing part of your life, instead of just a series of external events—good or bad reviews, deals made and lost, great or awful days at the keyboard. It's seeing your writing life as though it stretched to the horizon—all the ups and downs, hills and valleys, smoothing out from this lengthened perspective.

By slowing down, by taking the long view, you'll be better able to listen to your own instincts: such as writing urgently when possessed by it, or taking a workshop to jog the machinery into higher gear; but always with a sense of expansiveness, of adding on experiences and skills to the unfolding tapestry of your creative life, rather than a desperate chase after this year's hip writing technique, or bending your talent to this season's hot topic or genre.

Having the long view is being both energized and relaxed; enthusiastic and patient. It's knowing in the marrow of your bones this one paradoxical fact: Writing's been around a long time and will probably continue at least as long, and yet it always happens in the here and now.

The Shakers had a saying: "Live as though you had ten thousand years, or ten minutes." That's about just doing your work, day in and day out, forging your process out of the raw materials of your experience. Keeping your focus in the tension between building craft in the now and holding hope for the future.

For a writer, that's keeping the long view.

Part Four

THE REAL WORLD

I only write when I'm inspired,
and I see to it that I'm inspired
at nine o'clock every morning.

— PETER DE VRIES

Writing is easy—as long as you don't have a life.

Let's face it, real life—family, friends, bills, illness, deadlines, etc.—just gets in the way. (And I haven't even mentioned valet parking, the weather, politics, and agents.) When you consider the daily whirlwind of activities a writer has to negotiate, from dental visits and carpooling to buying birthday presents and getting the dog groomed, it's a miracle anything gets written at all. In fact, it's a miracle that anything has ever been written since the beginning of time.

Of course, I'm being facetious—but only slightly. Writers, in company with every other type of artist, dwell in the real world. Livings have to be made, food has to be purchased, rent and mortgages have to be paid, children have to be raised. There are friendships to sustain, bosses to appease, and relatives to endure.

And decisions to be made. Where to send the kids to school. What homeowners' insurance to buy. What to do about Aunt Marie, now that Uncle George is gone. Is this neighborhood still safe? Do I really need bifocals? You want me to be buried *where?*

Not to mention the thoughts, ideas, and feelings writers live with every day. Call them the subtext of daily life. The hurts, the resentments, the illusions, the pipe dreams, the doubts, the fears, the misunderstandings. What did she mean by that? Did I say that right? Who does he think he is, anyway? I'm such an idiot, why can't I make this work? If only I were smarter, more talented, more together, more . . . something. Hell, why did I check my stocks this morning? Where did I put that notebook? My back's going out again, I know it. Gotta concentrate. I'll start with that scene in the third act. After the mail comes. Geez, I gotta call my mother this week—*that's* another three sessions in therapy. Has anybody seen my notebook? No, the *other* one . . . Christ!

See what I mean? Real life—the cacophonous, constantly shifting yet relentlessly repetitive series of moments that make up a writer's day—is an omnipresent partner in the writing experience, a constant companion, and the only playing field in town. Real life is where a writer lives.

There *are* alternatives. Writers throughout history have sought solitude in which to write. Monks like Thomas Merton, essayists like May Sarton, novelists and screenwriters who rent cabins in the woods, or motel rooms in the Mojave, or villas in Spain. I know a playwright who works alone six months of the year in a fire lookout in Northern California.

But I would argue that even such solitude can't rescue the writer from the restrictions of real life, if we define "real life" merely as a person's lived experience. Besides, the choice to live alone, or without personal ties of any kind, also has a price tag: its own set of social, psychological, and pragmatic concerns. In other words, to quote a somewhat gloomy friend of mine, "Nobody escapes the existential dilemma."

On that cheery note, I'd like to offer three suggestions to help writers deal with the reality of writing in the real world. The first two are pretty conventional.

Structure time to write, and make it a fixed, regular time. The discipline of structure can have a surprisingly liberating effect on one's writing. To paraphrase Thomas Carlyle, "We must have order in our lives to go crazy in our work."

The second suggestion is merely to risk stepping back from life's distractions and regrouping. Go on a two-week retreat. Cancel all lunches and appointments. To whatever extent possible, exit the duties and responsibilities of your life for just a brief time—even if it's only an afternoon—and get back to your authentic core. Eliminate the background noise and see what's there. Because sometimes, as Andre Gregory says in *My Dinner With Andre,* "You've just got to cut out the noise."

My third and last suggestion is the most radical of all: Do nothing. Because, in reality, there's nothing *to* do about it. This is your life, the only playing field in town—your life, your thoughts, your memories, your frustrations, your dreams and hopes, your loves and hates.

What all of it means is best left to philosophers and theologians. What it means to me is, Wow, you have plenty to write about. All that stuff going on, and not enough hours in the day—or space in your imagination—to get to it.

Which means, I guess, you better get started. Tomorrow morning would be good.

The Pitch

Pitching your ideas is one of the realities of the writing life. Whether you're hawking a three-part series on forest conservation to the editor of your local paper or trying to sell a TV sitcom idea to NBC, you're part of a time-honored tradition of writers offering the promise of their talent to someone with the money to pay for it.

I know this aspect of the writing life quite well. When I worked in TV and film, I had to take meetings. Lots of them. Something like a thousand, over eighteen years. Most were pitch meetings, selling my ideas, my craft, *myself* to others.

But before I talk about the issues involved in pitching one's work, from my own experience and that of my clients, let me get my favorite "Pitch from Hell" story out of the way:

A producer and I were pitching a film at a big studio. We met with two executives, a male and a female, late on a Friday afternoon (already we were in trouble). About halfway through the meeting, *he* left to take an urgent call. Moments later, *she* excused herself to go to the rest room.

They never came back.

After waiting about twenty minutes, the producer and I sort of wandered the halls, peeking into empty cubicles. We figured each exec thought the other would cover the rest of the meeting. In any case, the place was deserted.

As we drove off the lot, I said to the producer, "Gee, they missed the best part of my pitch." Only I said it somewhat more colorfully.

Pitching is something that comes up constantly in my practice. At the very least, for most writers, it's a difficult and often dispiriting experience; for some, it's literally terrifying.

To deal with this, most writers I know develop little tricks or techniques to get them through the process. Some memorize the entire pitch (and pray nobody interrupts them); some have arcane theories as to how long to talk about each character or plot point; others believe in researching the professional (and sometimes personal) successes of the people they're pitching to, hoping to flatter their egos. Toward the further end of the spectrum we find hypnosis, relaxation tapes, and lucky socks.

My problem with these strategies, even the ones that appear to work, is that they're all an attempt to hide the writer. He or she "hides" behind the pitching technique, using it as a shield against what might emerge in the meeting. By that, I don't mean its professional outcome; I'm referring to the feelings that might be set off within the writer.

Samuel Johnson said, "Adversity introduces a man to himself." Likewise, I think pitch meetings introduce a writer to himself or herself. That's what makes them so frightening for so many people.

Years ago, I had a client, a feature writer for a national magazine, who suffered terrible anxiety before every pitch. No matter how strongly he felt about the idea he was proposing, how solidly constructed the story, the pitch rarely went well. Then, during a session about some difficult aspects of his personal life, he blurted out, "It's as though every event defines who I am."

A potent realization for him, and one that we saw applied as well to his fears about pitching. He experienced a pitch meeting as an event that ultimately defined how okay he was, how acceptable, perhaps even how entitled he was to be there. His defense against the powerful feelings of shame that might emerge if he failed was to work harder on the story, prepare more diligently, practice the pitch with friends, etc.

What he needed to do instead—which became the focus of our work together—was to *challenge the underlying assumption;* namely, that if the pitch didn't result in a sale, this defined him as unacceptable or inadequate.

Every pitch meeting, like every human encounter, is a relational event. We bring all our emotional baggage into that room—our performance anxiety, the meanings we give to failure and success, the requirement we may have felt in our families to be the "best and the brightest."

(Or the reverse. I recall a client who often sabotaged her performance in meetings, replaying her parents' injunction when she was a child not to show off or draw undue attention to herself because it might make others "feel badly about themselves.")

I think it's important for writers to explore what's underlying their fears and expectations about pitching so that they can develop better tools for alleviating the more painful aspects of the experience.

But it's also important to remember that pitching is a difficult task for just about everyone. To convey what's in your mind and heart is hard enough, let alone convincing someone to pay for it. It's practically a recipe for anxiety.

However, as Rollo May reminded us, anxiety is a necessary component of any creative act. Which even pitching can be, in the right circumstances, when our fears are accepted with humor and compassion and our convictions and enthusiasms can be engaged.

And the other guy hangs around long enough to see it.

Rejection

At some point early on in a writer's life, he or she has to come to terms with rejection. After over twenty years as a working writer, I know *I* certainly have—I hate it.

Occasionally I'll read about some writer whose personal philosophy is so well integrated into his life that he sees having his work rejected as just another event, one bead on a long string of similar beads; in other words, the rejection has no more (nor less) meaning than having his work accepted.

I confess, I can only stand back and admire such creatures, and wonder what planet they come from.

Because frankly, when I toiled in the screenwriting vineyards, I wanted people not only to accept what I wrote, but like it. A lot. Hell, I wanted them to love it (even while acknowledging the well-known truism that, at a certain level, they couldn't love it enough).

On the other hand, having my work rejected was cause for *tsuris* of near-biblical proportions—the familiar gnashing of teeth, rending of garments, etc. On one such occasion, a friend of mine looked at me and said, somewhat testily, "For God's sake, don't take it personally."

"How should I take it?" I replied. "*Im*personally?"

That, in a nutshell, is the paradox of rejection. It isn't intended as personal, but it's impossible not to experience it that way.

Let me give you an example. Years ago, on staff at a popular sitcom, I joined the producers in a casting session, auditioning actresses for a guest shot on the show. After seeing about a dozen read for the part, we chose one.

Later, I happened to overhear a couple of the others walking away, dejected.

"I should've looked hotter," one of them said.

"I overplayed that last scene," said another.

I'd heard similar laments from actors and actresses before, of course. "If only I'd done this, or that . . ." "If only I were thinner, prettier . . ." "If only, if only . . ."

What made it even more ironic in this case was the fact that we'd cast *this* particular actress because it was getting close to lunchtime and we were all hungry. As it turned out, all the actresses had been reasonably competent, so we just picked the next one who wasn't taller than the show's star and made tracks for the studio commissary.

Our agenda—in this case, hunger—could never have been known or predicted or prepared for by the others auditioning.

The same is true for writers. In my experience, not only is it a mystery why certain good scripts and stories get rejected; often it's a total mystery why they get accepted. I don't have a writer client who hasn't been perplexed when something he or she considers a lesser work is bought, while something he or she feels represents better work is consistently rejected.

As my anecdote about the audition demonstrates, the agenda of the marketplace—the sometimes incomprehensible, ever-changing, and often-maddening needs of publishers, agents, and studios—is out of your control, and not about you.

Therefore, their rejection of material you submit to them is not some injury personally directed at you.

However, as I said before, your experience of the rejection is personal. In fact, it can't be anything else.

So let yourself be angry, frustrated, even grief stricken. After all, as a somewhat kinder, gentler friend of mine once remarked, "when a painful thing happens, a period of mourning is appropriate."

But now the good news: Since you can't know (or control) the outcome of any pitch or submission, you're free to just do your work. Rather than shaping your writing to please others or to latch onto or anticipate the next trend, your best bet is to write about what excites and moves you, to make your growth as a writer the ultimate goal.

Darryl Hickman, a wonderful acting teacher, used to tell his students, "Keep giving them *you,* until you is what they want."

Not a bad piece of advice for writers, either. Stay true to yourself, and keep giving the marketplace your best until it takes it.

Remember, too, that rejection comes and goes, but so does acceptance. For a writer, over the long haul, it's mastery of your craft, wedded to the sheer love of doing it, that sustains.

And, finally, though the powers-that-be can accept or reject your work, you can do something they can't: write. The plain fact is, you are the sun, and the industry is the moon. It only shines by reflected light.

That Sinking Feeling

One of my favorite movie scenes is from James Brooks's *Broadcast News*. News producer Holly Hunter has just explained to a network exec all the reasons why his decision to elevate William Hurt's character to anchorman is a bad idea. The exec listens, then says sarcastically, "It must be wonderful to be the smartest person in the room."

"No," she replies, "it's awful."

I think of this exchange whenever I'm working with a screenwriter client caught in a particularly thorny patch of Development Hell. Usually, my client's being bombarded with notes by the director, producer, or development executive; suggestions that—no matter how well intentioned—will end up causing more problems than they solve.

Recently, I've come up with a clinical term for what the writer experiences during such meetings. I call it TSF, or That Sinking Feeling.

TSF is that slowly unfolding awareness in the pit of your stomach that what's being pitched in the room *will not work;* that the more excited everybody becomes about the new suggestions, the more you see the mountain of torturous effort and twisted logic involved in executing them; and that nothing you're going to do or say will change anybody's mind.

Every writer suffers from TSF at various times in a career. It's as virulent as the common cold, and about as inevitable. (One of its main symptoms, as previously discussed, is a powerful feeling of identification with that kid in the fairy tale about the Emperor's new clothes. An ancillary symptom is just slow-building dread.)

I recall one distinctive bout with TSF from my own screenwriting days. I was on the second draft of a comedy feature, working with a new producer at a big studio. Toward the end of a typically grueling notes meeting, the producer suddenly says, out of left field, "I have a great idea for Charlie [the script's second lead character]. Think Sam Kinison."

The late Sam Kinison, you probably recall, was a wildly funny (though extremely politically *in*correct) stand-up comic. At the time, there was no question he was a rising star. He just sure as hell wasn't our "Charlie." I mean, not even close. I mean, it would have to be a different movie entirely—different story, tone, approach to humor—

I mean, there was *just no way*—

So naturally, the producer wouldn't budge. "Now go," he said, sending me out to write the third draft. "And remember, for Charlie—think Sam Kinison."

Driving home from the meeting, I had That Sinking Feeling. I knew, like I knew my own name, that I was going to spend six weeks tailoring the script to suit Sam Kinison; I also knew we were never going to *get* Sam Kinison; that the studio would hate the rewrite; that it was all a colossal waste of time and energy.

And that there wasn't a damn thing I could do about it.

This story is typical of the dozens I've heard in my office over the years. From journalists told to make soul-chilling cuts in their feature story. From novelists advised by their editors to exchange Chapter One for Chapter Three, or to make a son into a daughter, or to give the blind kid an experimental drug at the end that restores his sight. One client, a poet, was asked by her editor to change all her commas to dashes, because "it worked for Emily Dickinson."

The problem with struggling against That Sinking Feeling is that the writer often has to work against his or her own instincts to accomplish the rewrite task. Author Frank McShane was talking about Hollywood in the following quote, but I think the sentiment rings true for all writers: "[When] they separate the writer from his unconscious, what's left is mere performance."

Which brings me back to Holly Hunter's line in *Broadcast News*. Because it *is* awful being the smartest one in the room.

Yes, I'm saying it out loud. In print. Writers are the smartest people in the room. Any room. Anywhere in town.

By "smartest," I don't mean writers are always right. But I do feel writers bring the most highly developed and articulated sense of story and character to a project. Plus, because a writer lives daily with the story—has an intimate relationship with its every beat, nuance, plot point, etc.—he or she is most suited to protecting and enhancing those elements that make the story work.

Not that that matters much in the overall scheme of things.

It's a situation guaranteed to make writers crazy: hired for that special, ephemeral skill that only writers bring to the table—then usually prevented from utilizing that gift to the fullest. No wonder writers come down with That Sinking Feeling.

However, there *is* compensation. I don't mean financial, though there is often that. I mean the value of the struggle itself.

Over the years, in my work with writers, I've grown to admire their attempts to stay connected with their deepest ideals and convictions, to tell the stories they want to tell. In spite of the odds, most writers resist being separated from the unconscious, the seedbed of their imagination.

Yes, it's a relentless struggle. Yes, the odds are tough. And yes, you can wrack up a lot of injuries battling That Sinking Feeling every damn day.

But who knows? Maybe that's just the price you pay for being the smartest one in the room.

Reinventing Yourself

In the real world, I feel it's important for writers to reinvent themselves as they move through their careers. And not merely for pragmatic reasons—the changing demands of the marketplace, the fear of being "typed" as a writer, and so on. I think it's important as an element of creative growth.

As I said earlier, my favorite quote for writers comes from Ray Bradbury: "There is only one type of story in the world—*your* story." And while I believe this is true, I also know this story has many chapters, lived and imagined.

What I mean is, as people and as writers we have many selves, many roles—parent, mate, sibling, friend. In the same way that we exist in a matrix of relationships, writers live in the matrix of imagined worlds of experience. We can be in the minds of serial killers and suburban moms, scientists and cartoonists, priests and pickpockets.

If we can imagine it, we can be it; we can write it.

And the process of expanding our creative vision can occur within the same medium, or by striking out on a new one—

perhaps then to return to familiar territory with renewed vigor. Many screenwriters write novels; sitcom writers do plays; playwrights publish essays. (To take reinvention to its extreme, one writer, Václav Havel, became president of his nation.)

So, how does a writer go about reinventing himself or herself? Here's a clue: In describing Zen training, Shunryu Suzuki said it was like emptying all the furniture and knick-knacks out of a room. Then, if you wished, you could put them all back in. But with renewed awareness.

This mental "spring cleaning" is a prerequisite for reinventing yourself. It can be quite exhilarating to blow the dust off your preconceived notions of the type of writer you are. What you uncover might amaze and delight you, or even alarm you, but it'll certainly expand you.

Of course, there are risks to reinventing yourself, trying to write in different styles, about different issues. We're comfortable with the familiar in our writing, especially if we've had any success with it—just as the public is more comfortable with the expected from their favorite authors. John Le Carre's only nonspy novel was a disappointment to his readers. And when Neil Simon adapted Chekhov for his play *The Good Doctor,* a theatergoer reportedly remarked at intermission, "This isn't Neil Simon."

On the other hand, risks are crucial to creative growth. Take Woody Allen's *Interiors*—not a huge success, perhaps, but a necessary step on the artistic road to *Manhattan* and *Hannah and Her Sisters.* The benefits of reinventing yourself as a writer go hand in hand with the appreciable risks, as with all growth experiences.

There's also this interesting paradox: The exploration of self that's necessary to reinvent your writing often helps

113

clarify the issues and themes about which you've always written.

Think of Paddy Chayefsky. After his success with *Marty,* he became worried that people thought of him as too "street," too engaged in the language and concerns of the "common man." As a result, he deliberately stretched as a writer, in both style and content, and in memorable fashion: *The Americanization of Emily, Hospital, Network.* Still, though the language (and IQ levels) of his characters was radically different from his earlier ones, he explored the same issues of alienation, pop culture, and social class. Is it that far a journey from mocking the popularity of Mickey Spillane in *Marty* to parodying the public's appetite for trash news in *Network?*

"There is only one type of story in the world—*your* story."

But there are limitless ways to tell it, and limitless opportunities to surprise ourselves with unexpected humor or darkness, pathos or bravado. If, as writers, we can relate to characters as disparate as Richard III and Seinfeld, Dr. Quinn and Hannibal Lecter, Gilligan and Grendel, then we have as many disparate selves within us waiting to be given voice.

Deadline Dread

Someone once said, "The problem with being a writer is that it's like always having homework due."

Which is as good a starting point as any for a discussion of deadlines, a fact of life in every writer's existence. But not every writer views a deadline in the same way. Like most facts of life, this aspect of writing holds a different meaning for different people. And most of these meanings were formed years ago, embedded in a writer's childhood experiences concerning ideas of expectation and performance.

For most of my writer clients, a deadline is viewed with dread, the same pressure to deliver the goods that they experienced in school when homework was due, or a big final exam was to be given, or there was some try-out in team sports. They experience the same fears of failure, or concerns that they would somehow fall short of their own and others' expectations. For some—then and now—the deadline represents the date at which long-held beliefs in their own inadequacy and unworthiness are finally confirmed. The approaching deadline is like the ticking clock in *High Noon*.

We're all familiar with this "deadline dread" and the stereotypical way writers cope: procrastination, which can take the form of household chores, distracting social activities, or just anxious fretting. Experienced procrastinators spend hours "researching" on the net, or rewriting again and again the stuff they've managed to produce so far.

Regardless of coping strategies, the dread is the same: the potential danger of self-exposure; that once written and handed in, the finished product exposes us as inadequate, untalented, or unentitled.

On the other hand, there's a smaller group among my clients for whom a deadline, despite its attendant anxiety, is an absolute must. These writers feel they need the prod of a deadline, or else they'd never finish the work (or even start it!). While this may seem an acceptable state of affairs, I think it's a good idea to investigate a bit further. Often, there's a kind of negative reinforcement in this line of thinking, the meaning being that the writer feels himself or herself to be a lazy, unmotivated worker who needs to be whipped into compliant productivity by the authority of an imposed deadline. As a novelist client confessed, "Without a deadline to meet, I'd go all to hell . . . I mean, I'd just screw around, not accomplishing anything."

A screenwriter in my practice put it this way: "A deadline just puts the gun to my head . . . if I don't get the damned thing in on time, BOOM!"

There's a pleasant way to spend the next twenty or thirty years of one's life!

Regardless of how you view deadlines, they offer an opportunity to explore and maybe temper the self-critical, self-shaming ways you might be viewing yourself. When the next deadline for a writing project looms, take some time to investigate your feelings about it. Look under the almost automatic response of anxiety and dread to see what kind of message you're sending yourself. Do you feel the same way with every deadline, or does it change depending on the type of project, the person you're delivering it to, your perceived (or their explicit) level of expectation? How are these ways of experiencing deadlines similar to the ways you felt as a child in your family, a student at school? Whose authority and judgment evoked these feelings the most? Do you experience your project's potential reader—the producer, editor, agent, etc.—in some similar way?

By exploring and illuminating these issues, writers can sometimes get the perspective needed to ease the grip that deadline dread has on them. Moreover, you can develop coping strategies based on these understandings; for example, if you use deadlines as a motivator but suffer anxiety, you can gain some measure of control by setting a series of private, personal deadlines for yourself, points at which you not only see where you are on the project but also take some time to assess your feelings about it, identify various creative and emotional concerns, and regroup. In other words, become your *own* authority regarding your writing process, instead of merely being vulnerable to that imposed from outside.

Let's face it. As long as there are writers—and writing assignments—there'll be deadlines. How we deal with them, how we weave them into the fabric of our working lives, is up to us. In fact, as I once suggested to a client, "You could keep a journal about it . . . maybe jot down the issues you think deadlines evoke for you."

"Can I bring it in to show you?" he asked.

"Sure. Our next session, if you'd like."

"Great." He grinned. "A deadline."

Three Hard Truths

In my practice, I try to help writers come to terms with a variety of issues associated with writing. Together, we endeavor to explore and challenge their expectations, their fears and fantasies, the very meanings they assign to the peaks and valleys of the writer's life. Hopefully, the most painful, most debilitating aspects of a client's self-experience can be illuminated and integrated. At the very least, writers can learn coping strategies to help them coexist with many of the internal conflicts that plague them.

That said, there's another aspect of the writing life that exists over and apart from our experience *of* writing. These are aspects of writing itself that cannot be "resolved" or "integrated," and certainly not "cured." They are intrinsic to writing. They're what I call the Three Hard Truths about writing.

The First Hard Truth: Writing is a craft, as well as an art, and that craft takes time to develop. Forget genius, forget inspiration. It takes time—measured not in weeks or months, but years. Hemingway said, "Write a million words." He wasn't kidding.

Time . . . page after page, draft after draft, month after month, year after year. Scenes and more scenes, characters and events and images, discarding and changing and shuffling and reshuffling, and throwing it all out and starting over again. That's the writer's commitment, and that requires time. Or, should I say, a lifetime?

The Second Hard Truth: With every new project, you have to teach yourself how to write it. Each new piece of writing is unique unto itself. To put it another way, you and the thing you're about to write are encountering each other for the first time. The script or novel or play you wrote last year, or last month, can't help much, regardless of its similarities in style or content to the new project. For one thing, you're in a different place emotionally, creatively, perhaps even professionally. You bring a different set of feelings and attitudes, whether or not you can even articulate these to yourself. Even if you're trying consciously to re-create what you've done before, it's not really possible.

This is not, by the way, a bad thing. In fact, it's the lifeblood of creativity, this always-newness. It's also one of writing's finer paradoxes: For centuries, writers have labored to explore and explicate what Faulkner called "the eternal verities," yet every time a writer sits down to write, it's new. A wise writer knows this, and revels in it. So that, ultimately, regardless of your years of experience as a writer, or your level of success, you come to the blank page (or screen) with anticipation for what you'll discover, in effect, as a beginner. To quote Suzuki's famous advice, "In the beginner's mind, there are many possibilities; in the expert's mind, there are few."

The Third Hard Truth: Writing carries no guarantees. You can never know how a piece of writing will turn out— whether it'll be any good, whether anyone will like it, whether it will ever be sold. Writing, to put it flatly, is all about risk.

No matter how hard you work, how studiously you apply yourself, no matter even how innately talented you may feel you are, there are no guarantees. You can't know the outcome of any writing endeavor. Writing, like life (and baseball, for that matter, or marriage, or politics), is totally unpredictable. Every time you start a new writing project, you're sailing off into uncharted waters. Whether you make it to shore depends on a hundred variables, few of which (outside of effort and commitment) are under your control. And when you finally get there, when the novel or script is finished, it may fall far short of your hopes.

On the other hand, it may not. The writing may sing, the story might very well quicken the heart. You may just pull off the alchemist's trick and have some real gold on your hands. But you can't know until you get there. You just can't know.

Well, there they are, the Three Hard Truths. To be honest, my chest has gotten progressively tighter as I've been writing this. My breathing, I swear to God, is shallow. These hard truths scare the hell out of *me!* They seem so implacable, so nonnegotiable, so . . . well . . . hard. (I'm beginning to wish I'd written this chapter about something else, like puppies. Or rainbows. Anything!)

Besides, these Three Hard Truths aren't really Truths at all. Let's face it, they're just my ideas, one man's opinion. . . . I could be way off base here.

But I don't think so.

Part Five

PAGE FRIGHT

———

Traveler, there is no path.
Paths are made by walking.
—ANTONIO MACHADO

What is it about writing that makes it so terrifying? There are as many different answers as there are writers, and as many different ways to deal with our fears.

In this part, I'd like to focus on an aspect of the writer's life that, at first glance, seems among the most mundane—up there with learning the computer and remembering to enclose a self-addressed, stamped envelope. I'm talking about a writer's habits, both good and bad.

The key to managing our writing fears, our "page fright," is craft; however, craft doesn't just emerge from an accumulation of months or years of work, but from the development of good writing habits. And, at the same time, some advice to help recognize and diminish the bad ones.

Gumption Traps

"I like the word 'gumption' because it's so homely and so forlorn and so out of style it looks as if it needs a friend."

The preceding quote is from *Zen and the Art of Motorcycle Maintenance*, by Robert Pirsig (one of the real must-read books in a person's life, in my opinion, as I'll discuss later). Anyway, he was talking in this section of the book about problem solving, and how one of the personal tools required is plain, old-fashioned gumption.

Certainly I think gumption is a trait crucial to a successful, satisfying writing career. Gumption is the "get up and do it" portion of the creative process. By which I don't mean "Just do it," in the mindless exhortation of those Nike ads. I'm referring to the sustained, meaningful, and concerted *effort* required to write.

Many of my clients think talent, wedded with desire, are the twin engines of a writing career. And, of course, these are both vital to the writing process—in conjunction with craft and, as I've stressed repeatedly, access to one's feelings.

But gumption is something else. It has to do with will, with determination, with the exhilaration of doing. However, as Pirsig points out, gumption can be so easily undermined by ego, boredom, and impatience.

By ego, he refers to a belief that you have nothing more to learn. Boredom results from no longer seeing things in a fresh light. Impatience often comes from underestimating the time it takes to complete the task.

These problems, among others, he sees as "gumption traps," things that can really let the air out of your ability to apply a sustained effort.

Now, from my perspective working with writers, the important lesson about gumption is to be careful what you use to feed it. All too often writers lapse into shaming themselves as a goad to work harder. Or, as one client told me recently, regarding his work ethic, "Don't worry, I can always 'guilt' myself into working."

Gumption rarely arises from shame or guilt. But resentment does; as do lethargy and depression. And even if you do manage to cajole, threaten, or in some other way force yourself to write, the result is usually a joyless experience. (And, often, so is reading the finished product!) Such negative reinforcement may get you to do the thing, and even get you through it. But you sure as hell won't want to do it again.

Gumption, as I see it, is about paying attention. Noticing your boredom or impatience, and exploring it. Why are you bored? Is it perhaps not anger? Or fear? Fear of what? As these impediments to sustained effort are illuminated and understood, movement occurs. As Pirsig writes, "A person filled with gumption is at the front of the train of his own awareness, watching to see what's up the track and meeting it when it comes."

Let's look at it from another angle. I mentioned before the Hindu belief that the secret of contentment lies in absorption. I think this is the key to gumption. Rather than seeing it as a function of a person's character, as embedded in the Judeo-Christian ethic, I conceptualize gumption as the natural sustained effort that arises out of being absorbed in a task. Then your energy reserves are boundless, because everything about the task—including your emotional responses to it—becomes interesting, worth noting and exploring.

Being absorbed in the task of writing, experiencing fully each thought or feeling that emerges moment by moment, including your frustration, boredom, etc., enhances your sense of aliveness. In short, the more absorbed you are, the more you fuel the gumption that allows you to sustain the effort.

But what if, despite your best efforts, at some point in your work you're just stuck, lost? I'll let Pirsig offer a final thought: "Then, what you have to do is slow down, and go over ground that you've been over before to see if things you thought were really important were really important, and then you have to . . . well . . . just stare at the thing. Just live with it for a while. Watch it the way you watch a line when fishing, and before long you'll get a little nibble, a little fact or idea asking in a timid, humble way if you're interested in it. That's the way the world keeps on happening. Be interested in it."

Procrastination

As I was assembling this book, I knew I wanted to write a chapter about procrastination. Except that I didn't seem able to write it. Or even to start.

I'd cleared off my desk, made a fresh pot of coffee, flipped on the word processor—and sat staring at it. I figured it was time to have one of those frank, unsparing conversations with myself.

"Weren't you going to write about procrastination?"

"Yeah. I just haven't gotten around to it yet."

"Very cute. Meanwhile, your book comes to a screeching halt."

"But I haven't figured out how to open the chapter. You have to grab 'em with the first line, ya know."

"I've heard that."

"Maybe I should check my files. I've got all sorts of great stuff in here. Jokes, anecdotes, news clippings . . . Hey, here's that letter from Jim back in Pittsburgh. Geez, I gotta send him a note, or an e-mail or something—"

"You can do that later. For now, you've got work to do."

"Don't worry, I'm on it. Right after the mail comes."

"Give me a break, will ya? C'mon, we're both sitting down, the computer screen's blank and waiting—"

"What do you mean, 'we'? *I'm* the one who's gotta write this thing. You get to just hang around, badgering me."

"*Somebody* has to. Besides, I didn't say a word yesterday, when you spent the morning browsing in Dutton's Bookstore instead of doing this chapter."

"You didn't have to. The whole time I was there, the fact that I wasn't writing hung in the air like stale tobacco smoke. I started to imagine that everybody *knew*. I couldn't make eye contact with Dave, behind the counter. I was afraid he'd come over and say, 'So how's that chapter on procrastination coming?' It ruined the whole experience for me."

"Then you should've come back and written the damn thing."

"Brilliant. If I could've done *that*, I wouldn't be procrastinating, would I? I'd be writing."

"Look, I'm just trying to help. In fact, I think I'm doing a helluva job."

"You've gotta be kidding. Based on what?"

"Based on the fact we're halfway through this thing already—"

"*Again* with the 'we' stuff. Though, now that you mention it . . ."

"You're welcome. See, all we've done is use the same technique you often suggest to your clients. Instead of obsessing about the fact that they're procrastinating, they should *write* about it. As a dialogue with themselves. Or a story. Even a letter to themselves."

"That's right. If a client writes about his feelings about

procrastinating, the underlying doubts and fears may emerge, as well as the meaning he gives them. Say, for example, that he shouldn't even be trying to write. Or that if he does, it won't be good enough. Whatever. Hopefully, as these self-defeating meanings are examined, the writer can better understand his procrastination as a kind of defense mechanism. That he procrastinates as a way to avoid discovering some imagined 'truth' about himself."

"Uh-huh. Remember that screenwriter client who tried the technique, writing page after page about her procrastination issues? Ultimately, she got so bored doing *that*, it just became easier to write the damned script!"

"Well, it worked, didn't it? For a writer struggling with procrastination, the important thing to remember is that *writing anything* is by definition the act of overcoming it."

"And by that you mean? . . ."

"I once had a client who figured out ingenious ways to procrastinate—I mean, forget house cleaning and file cataloging. This woman organized block parties in her neighborhood, kept up mailing lists for her alumni association, spent days trying to invent a new coffee blend for her local Starbucks—"

"I get it. So?"

"So I had her write down what she was doing instead of writing . . . each activity, her problems with it, her feelings about it. At some point, she began to see herself as a character doing these things, then writing about that character. Soon, this all turned into a novel."

"Interesting. By the way, have you noticed we're just about finished with this chapter?"

"But I was just getting started. Ironic, isn't it? All that

time and effort spent procrastinating, and now that I'm writing, I don't want to stop."

"Now, what have we learned from this, Grasshopper?"

"I'll have to get back to you. Don't forget, I'm in the middle of a book here."

Patience

I remember, as a kid, an embroidered sampler my aunt had on her living room wall. It read, "Lord, grant me patience—but hurry!"

I think of this saying often, especially when working with writer clients. Not surprising. After all, commercial writing—books, magazines, TV, and film—is a present-tense industry. In recent years, its motto has shifted from "What have you done lately?" to "What's next—and make it fast, line two is blinking."

As a result, patience—with oneself, one's work, and, more important, one's *way* of working—is a somewhat devalued commodity, particularly among those who ought to know better—writers themselves.

Nowadays, few writers are advised to cultivate patience. There's a lot of pressure to just write, to get it out there, to strive mightily to come up with the next high concept. We live in a competitive, consumerist culture, and there's a tremendous urgency to perform. A virtue like patience—sort of in the same homey, humble category as gumption—can get lost in the manic rush to produce material.

It seems, too, that the word *patience* has lost some of its calming assurance, its reference to longevity, endurance, and the slow growth of technical skill. Rather than thinking of it as the quality that enables a writer to explore his or her material, growing more competent by small, even measures, patience has taken on the attributes of a necessary evil. When a client who's struggling in his career or with his creative process tells me, through clenched teeth, that he "needs to have more patience," what he's referring to is an arms-folded, foot-tapping-nervously-on-the-floor kind of *im*patience, waiting for things to get better.

When seen in this way, having patience becomes the sorry equivalent of having to eat your spinach; it's supposed to be good for you—it's a damned virtue, isn't it?—but nobody really likes it.

Patience, then, rather than having a calming, protective function, becomes strained, a tortured version of "waiting your turn" until you, too, make it as a writer.

Stephen Levine, a well-regarded meditation teacher, once described the cause of suffering as, simply, "wanting things to be otherwise." I think this is the key to understanding the value of patience for a writer. If a writer thinks she is being patient by, symbolically, gritting her teeth and waiting for "things to be otherwise," then she will in fact only add to her suffering.

Believe me, I understand the temptation to envision patience in this self-defeating manner, especially given the competitive environment writers find themselves in now.

Write more, write faster, writer funnier, write bigger—these are the admonitions writers hear every day. So I'm probably in the minority when I suggest that writers rethink the concept of patience, not as a virtue one has to swallow, like the aforementioned spinach, but as a qualitative state of mind to be nurtured—for its own sake—in oneself.

Writers, like everyone else in contemporary life, seem in a great rush to "get somewhere." But without truly staying "where you are"—without being with your thoughts, feelings, and impulses, and really inhabiting them—what is there about you that can emerge to inform your writing? Getting somewhere is meaningless if the writing that results leaves your authentic self behind.

In the film *Chariots of Fire*, someone says, regarding Eric Liddle's unwillingness to race on the Sabbath, that the boy's faith needs to be honored; that the Olympics officials made a mistake when they "sought to sever his running from himself." In the same way, you can't separate the writer from the writing. And you can't know yourself—you the person, you the writer—without patience. Patience encourages and underscores the notion that your career is not only a life-long pursuit, but a daily connection to your experience of living it.

Moreover, patience builds faith in one's craft, because craft results from the slow accumulation of skill—that is, the mistakes, the breakthroughs, the false starts, the one-step-forward-two-steps-back rhythm that *is* the writing life. The cultivation of patience—not as a "waiting for things to change" but as a state in and of itself—leads to awareness and self-acceptance, necessary components of artistic command.

Rather than being in such a hurry to get somewhere,

writers are better served by exploring more fully where they are now—and that requires patience.

In other words, if I were making a sampler to hang on the wall, mine would read, "Lord, grant me patience—and take Your time about it."

Perspective

A few chapters back, I wrote about the wisdom for a writer in taking the long view regarding his or her career; that is, remembering that the ups and downs will smooth out over the years, and that a consistent, long-term commitment to artistic growth and the development of craft is what provides the ultimate satisfaction. In the same chapter, however, I also suggested that writing only occurs in the here and now.

I want to explore this seeming paradox, particularly in light of a session I had recently with a novelist client. She was about a third of the way through a new novel, one that represented a huge leap in terms of scope and content, and she was in the throes of powerful feelings of doubt and confusion. Would all the elements of plot, character, and theme come together successfully? Had she the talent, stamina, and craft to keep at it, when the end was so many months, maybe even a year or two, away? What if the whole thing collapsed, half-finished, a painful and fruitless waste of months of work?

"If only I could step back from all of it," she said. "Get some perspective."

"You *will* be able to have perspective," I said. "When it's finished. You can see the thing as a whole."

"Yeah, but I want that perspective *now.*" She gave me a wry smile, but I knew she was only half-kidding.

As we struggled with her conflicts about the novel, I kept thinking of something Kierkegaard said: "Life can only be understood backwards; unfortunately, we have to live it forward." What he meant is that, in hindsight, the choices and events in our life probably form a recognizable pattern, or possess a kind of thematic logic. But embedded as we are in our moment-to-moment daily life, we haven't the perspective to grasp fully the implications of decisions, behaviors, and events we take part in.

I realized this was the dilemma for my client. Embedded in the daily struggle to make this scene work, that character come to life; to create the hoped-for mood and tone as the pages of the novel flowed together, she was forced to stay in the here and now. The more she took creative risks, the more she mined her own feelings and experiences to give meaning and weight to her characters and scenes, the more fully in the world of the novel she dwelt. In other words, she couldn't see the forest for the trees.

The hell of it is, good writing *is* only about the trees, not the forest. You're planting your trees, one at a time, day after day—until, after many weeks or months, you get to stand back and look it over as a whole and say, "So *this* is what the forest looks like. I'll be damned."

The plain fact is, the more fully engaged you are with your writing process, the less perspective you can have. "The eye cannot see itself," as the Buddhists say. Now here's why I think that's a good thing.

As my client and I investigated her concerns about the

novel, it became clear that the perspective she desired was in fact a yearning for control. Her novel represented a real creative and financial risk. Elements of the story were autobiographical, and intensely painful, and were played out against a large and colorful canvas, spanning decades.

The difficulty of the task daunted her and exposed her to painful feelings of inadequacy. Even more shaming was the notion that attempting a novel like this revealed the depth of her pride and grandiosity, traits that were particularly frowned upon in her immediate family.

Given such a set of concerns and associations, who *wouldn't* want to have control over the writing? To be absolutely certain that the book was working, the writing was going well, that the novel would be a critical and financial success? In short, that the end result would justify the pains of its creation.

As my client worked her way toward this understanding, she saw the inherent contradiction in what she yearned for. If she was going to risk writing the novel, which meant living daily with her doubts and fears about it, she'd have to give up the idea of perspective. Which, in this case, meant control over the outcome.

"But only in the heat of the writing," I reminded her. "There does come a time when it's necessary and appropriate to take perspective, and that's when the book's done. Remember, writing may occur in the here and now, but editing takes place in the there and then."

"I know," she said. "Thank God."

By session's end, she was ready to go home and risk planting another tree. For my money, that's as good as it gets.

In Praise of Goofing Off

Some people call it puttering, or screwing around, or just plain goofing off. Others, of a more kindly bent, call it daydreaming. Kurt Vonnegut uses the quaint old term "skylarking." Then there are the sanctimonious, uptight, nonwriter types who call it, simply, wasting time.

What I'm referring to, of course, is that well-known, rarely discussed but absolutely essential component of a successful writer's life—the *downtime,* when you're seemingly not doing anything of consequence, certainly not doing anything that pertains to that deadline you're facing, that short story you've been toiling over, that second draft that's pending.

The concept of downtime, or goofing off, is shrouded in mystery for one very simple reason: It infuriates the writer's spouse, family, business colleagues, and friends. Let's face it: They just don't get it.

Here you are, struggling with a rewrite that's due in two weeks, and your mate finds you spending precious hours looking out the window, or reading *The New Yorker,* or watching *His Gal Friday* for the fifteenth time. Not to mention the valuable potential writing time wasted repairing your old bicycle, cleaning out the garage, or organizing your bookshelves according to author and/or subject.

I know what you're thinking: The preceding examples look suspiciously like procrastination. I understand your confusion. But there's a very subtle difference between procrastination and creative, productive, process-nourishing goofing off.

Procrastination, as I see in my practice every day, is a product of a writer's inner conflicts around writing itself. Fears about failure, questions about one's sense of entitlement, doubts about competence, concern about the potential for shameful exposure. Writers procrastinate to avoid the pain of discovering what they feel will be inadequacies in their writing; and often, by extension, in themselves.

I remember, from my days as a screenwriter, the particular quality of experience that procrastinating brought to the most trivial and pleasant of diversions. Going to a movie, walking on the bluffs in Santa Monica, indulging in three-hour lunches with other writers—all these activities were tinged with anxiety, with the awareness that I should be *elsewhere,* back at my desk, writing. These were all things I was doing instead of writing, instead of grappling with problems in plot and character; instead, moreover, of examining what might be going on inside my head about my ability to solve these problems.

How different in feeling from goofing off, or skylarking, or puttering! In my experience, when a writer is working well, these same side activities—hanging pictures, reading, cleaning out your files—serve as an adjunct to writing, necessary downtime for allowing your thoughts to percolate, for letting a new idea simmer in the pot for a while. You're not rereading *The Sun Also Rises* for the umpteenth time instead of writing: You're allowing that part of your brain that creates to work unconsciously, filtering and sorting, selecting and discarding.

Equally important, I think, is that there are often analogies between nonwriting activities and the writing itself. Who's to say that cleaning out your desk isn't a way to help organize your thinking? That talking with other writers about their ideas, goals, and troubles isn't a way to help reinvigorate your own writing ambitions or to get perspective on a particular concern? Certainly, reading others is a path to clarifying your own writing goals and issues. As I'll talk about in a later chapter, I've tried to read *The Great Gatsby* every year, just to revel in its jewel-like prose and striking emotional economy; just as an aid to my own writing.

Finally, one salient fact must be accepted: The writing process is damned *mysterious*. As a kid in parochial school, I was often chided by the nuns for gazing out the window, my attention who-knows-where, instead of focusing on the blackboard. I was a "day-dreamer," according to Sister Hillaire, the principal, in sharply worded notes routinely sent home to my parents. "Nothing good," she warned, "could come of this." (Nuns, I was to discover, could be melodramatic as hell.)

The point is, most writers start out as kids looking out the window, their heads in the clouds, their minds a million miles away, etc. But one person's daydreamer is another person's "writer-in-training." No matter how much we try, it's impossible to quantify the writing process. It's mysterious, even to writers, and it resists all attempts to explicate its secrets.

Which is why it's ultimately fruitless to try to explain to family and friends what you're doing when, instead of banging away at the keyboard, you're recataloging your CD collection. I suggest you just give them a wry, mysterious, genius-at-work smile, and go on about your business.

Writing about Dogs

One of my favorite *New Yorker* cartoons, by George Booth, depicts a tormented, obviously blocked writer sitting at his typewriter, crumpled paper strewn about, surrounded by literally dozens of dogs—napping, barking, hanging from the window sills, etc. The writer's wife stands in the doorway, glaring at him in weary disdain. "Write about dogs," she says.

Aside from its dark humor, the cartoon's truth is that this frustrated writer often doesn't see that a subject for his writing is right in front of him—the dogs; that is, the obvious elements that actually inhabit his life.

In my efforts to help writers develop a more benign and inclusive approach to accessing their creative gifts, I often suggest they follow one simple maxim: Work with what you're given. By that, I mean work with—and write from—your singular subjective experience of the actual elements of your life. And not just your particular feelings and thoughts, as I've argued before, but the tangible, concrete elements: your neighborhood, a row of trees, the peculiar shadow shapes made by your car in the moonlight, that three-day hospital stay, the way certain songs sound on old LPs instead of CDs. In other words, figuratively speaking, writing about dogs.

At a deeper level, I'm suggesting that writers practice *seeing*—I mean, really seeing the world around them, and allowing these concrete elements to be experienced in a fresh light by virtue of the degree of attention and reflection they inspire in you. (And I don't see this merely as a writing exercise. Diane Ackerman got a best-seller, *A Natural History of the Senses,* out of writing in depth about our five senses. Think, too, of Annie Dillard's *Pilgrim at Tinker Creek*. To me, it's a meditation on just paying attention.)

Nothing invigorates our writing—no matter what genre or what medium—like looking with fresh eyes, experiencing what's in our environment with all our senses. We're sensory beings, after all; in addition, we're meaning-makers. We give things meaning. Put the two together and you have the writer's true raw materials.

Think of how powerfully a particular smell can evoke strong memories of a meaningful event in your life. Let's say a certain stale, musty smell triggers a vivid memory of a childhood summer spent on a farm, playing in an old barn. Maybe it's when you first felt the pangs of adolescent love, or were given adult responsibilities, or developed an affinity for nature; maybe, as happened to a friend of mine, you came home to discover your parents were getting a divorce. That summer at the farm—alive again in all its colors and tones thanks to a single smell—was a sensory experience now embedded in a set of ideas, convictions, and feelings. It's a short leap from that smell, and the memory it triggers, to associations in your mind about who you are, what happened to you, how you think about things.

In the case of my friend, the memory of that summer on the farm has one specific meaning: Be wary of happiness; it means you're about to be blind-sided by some oncoming misfortune.

Sensory experience plus meaning. Like it or not, it's how we make sense of our lives.

As a writer, your job is to do this consciously and artfully, using craft and imagination as well as memory and reflection. To do this well, you have to pay attention.

Tolstoy said, "Love those whom God has put before you." The Tao is even more inclusive: "Love the Ten Thousand Things." In short, see—that is, love—everything. Don't just see everything and everybody in your experience as grist for the mill. To be a good writer, you must love the grist for its own sake.

What do I mean by this? To "love" the totality of what we experience is to accept all of our responses to it, to be enlivened by the variety of ways we experience events, good or bad, painful or joyful. The artist's task is to see every moment—and our reaction to it—as potentially interesting, challenging, and worthy of our creative participation.

Viewed from this perspective, a writer is never bored, never longs for things in his or her life to be more interesting, more exciting, more *something else* than they actually are. Except, of course, for when you *do* feel that way, in which case you should write about that boredom, or that longing. That's your grist for that particular day. It's working with what you're given.

Ultimately, it comes down to two choices: You can trip over the dog on your way to the office, where you fret and anguish at the keyboard waiting for the Big Idea to come to you—or you can write about the dog.

Going the Distance

I think it's a truism: The longer the writing project, the deeper and more debilitating the page fright. Here is where the narrative goes astray, the plot unravels, the theme becomes obscured; here is when the work peters out, slows for months at a time, or is even occasionally abandoned.

In other words, perhaps a writer's greatest challenge is going the distance.

In the early 1960s, there was a hot art-house movie called *The Loneliness of the Long Distance Runner.* I think of this film sometimes when trying to help clients working on long-form projects—plays, screenplays, novels, etc. The running analogy is a good one, because long-form writing is like running a marathon: It requires endurance, patience, a deep reserve of willpower and commitment, and an almost herculean ability to delay gratification.

(To continue the analogy, other kinds of writing might be likened to sprints—short stories, TV episodes, poems. Sprints require a burst of speed and power, the knock-out punch of a single idea or concept, and a quick build to an explosive finish.)

Where the long-form writer gets in trouble is in believing that he or she can maintain over the length of the project the same vigor and intensity that's brought to a shorter piece. Hence, when the work slows, or gets bogged down in exposition, or drifts off on tangents, the writer panics. His or her confidence flags. Enthusiasm drains away. The unfinished novel or screenplay is put away in a drawer, "just for a while," often never to be approached again.

To avoid this, here are some suggestions to help you "keep on keeping on" during those long, painful stretches that plague anyone writing a big project:

Pace yourself. As I said, it's a marathon, not a sprint. Twelve-hour days at the keyboard, living on pizza and Diet Coke, may get you through a short piece or rewrite that's on deadline, but for a novel or mini-series it's deadly: hard on your family, your vital organs, and your outlook on life.

Expect slow spots, things that don't work, and reverses. Long-form storytelling has its own rhythm, in the reading as well as the writing. The reader needs to take a breath, be reminded of plot points, given a break from unending action and/or revelation. So do you, the writer.

Like any extended trip, the journey through a novel or screenplay involves wrong turns, pleasant surprises off the beaten path, some reflective time to remind yourself why you're even taking this route, even return visits to places and events to see what further gold can be mined from them. Just keep reminding yourself that you're in this for the long haul, that there'll be good days and bad, pitfalls and peaks of inspiration, and then get on with it.

Take sidetrips. Stop occasionally to write a short piece—

an article or essay, a letter to the local Op-Ed section, e-mail to some friends, etc. This gives your long-form muscles some much-needed R&R and helps flex those short-form ones. Just because you're running a marathon doesn't mean you want to forget how to sprint.

* Limit contact with nonsupportive family and friends. A seemingly obvious suggestion, I'm always stunned at how often writer clients will reveal their creative concerns to the wrong people in their lives, folks whose own agendas— unconsciously or not—contribute to reinforcing the most self-defeating aspects of a writer's personality. Avoid such people like the plague. Turn off your phone's ringer, put a "condemned" sign outside your apartment building, assume a false identity and move to Cairo—whatever it takes!

* Don't rush the ending (just to get the damned thing finished). A hard temptation to resist, but you've got to try. There's no sense laboring over a piece for months, or even years, getting the narrative, characters, and tone just right, only to rush the thing to its climax because you're so relieved to finally see the end approaching. Let the reader—and you, too—enjoy the fruits of your labor; give yourself the luxury of bringing the same effort and care to making the most out of the conclusion. Do justice to your characters, your story—and to yourself.

* Finally, when the project is done, expect some postpartum blues. You've lived in the world of your novel, play, or screenplay for so long, it's familiar, the known. Despite its myriad problems and headaches, it's what you've called home for a long time. Believe me, after bitching about it the whole time you've been writing it, when it's finally finished you'll miss it.

Which is why, as hard as it is to write a long-form piece,

as vehemently as you swear that you'll never do it again, pretty soon you'll start thinking about a new one.

That's the funny thing about going the distance. Once you know you can do it, some part of you—some perverse part of you, no doubt—will want to do it again.

Just like with running a marathon. Or, perhaps, like the end of a long, painful relationship. You swear to anyone who'll listen that you'll never fall in love again. Then, one day, you see someone in a bookstore or at a party, and you say, "Hmmmm . . ."

It's kinda like that.

Part Six

THE REAL WORLD, PART II

There is no such thing as security.
There never has been.

— GERMAINE GREER

Over the years, as first a screenwriter and now a therapist working with writers, nothing has rankled me more than running into nonwriters at parties, weddings, class reunions, whatever, who claim to be interested in writing "someday." (For want of a better word, let's call these folks "civilians.")

In my own experience, most civilians—and I include some producers, agents, and editors in this group—are people who feel they *could* be writers, if they only had the time. They often believe the only thing that separates them from the professional writer is the luxury of those three or four hours a day that writers enjoy. (I once had a studio executive complain to me that if *he* had "hours free every day to think up dialogue and stuff," he'd get a lot more done than most writers he knew, and with a lot less whining and bitching, too. But he couldn't *do* this, of course, because he "had a real job," taking meetings, watching budgets, answering to unhappy superiors, etc.)

155

The preceding anecdote reveals something that even people outside of show business, publishing, or the arts believe about writing: that, seen from the civilian point of view, writing is essentially doable by anybody with an idea, a keyboard, and a disinclination to do legitimate work.

(And, yes, while it's true I did have a writer client who claimed he chose his career because it entailed "no heavy lifting," I like to think guys like him are in the minority.)

The truth is, anybody can have an idea. And almost any idea can be the foundation for a good script, short story, or novel. Regardless of how mundane or uneventful a life looks from the outside, each person has a story, an autobiographical narrative filled with almost operatic passions: loss, regret, love, tragedy, triumph. The whole magilla. The inclination, even the wistful yearning, to write about these things, to tell a story, is normal and understandable.

And, further, anybody can sit down at a keyboard and start writing it . . . for one day. That's the crux of the matter. *Anybody can be a writer for one day.*

In addition to the usual problems of talent, craft, and imagination, what makes the profession of writing so difficult is that it requires constancy. You have to do it every day, with consistency and will, just like any other occupation. Also, like any other job, you have to do it whether or not you feel like it some days, whether or not the work is going well, whether or not your efforts are being appreciated or even rewarded sufficiently. Writing for a living, like doing almost anything else, requires being a grown-up. Or at least acting like one.

Anybody can be a writer for one day. You sit down, you write some scenes, or even a whole story. Maybe you even think it's pretty good. Meaty, funny, trenchant, poignant.

Maybe you show it to people, friends and relatives at first, then risk giving it to some agent or editor you know.

Let's say the response is negative. You get lots of criticism, suggestions, unsolicited comments praising you for trying, but saying, as the joke goes, "keep your day job."

Let's say the response is positive. But still, you get lots of notes, some requests for changes. Maybe they even want more. More pages, more stories, more things like it. "More?" you ask. "You mean I have to do this again?"

If you're a real writer, living in the real world, the answer is "Yes, whether it works or it doesn't, you have to do this again. You have to sit down and hammer out story beats, character nuances, narrative turns. You have to fine-tune the rhythm and pacing, shore up the second act, heighten the conflict. And you have to do this with an eye on the market-place, and yet stay fresh and original. You have to do this while keeping your agent interested, your family fed, and your sanity intact. And you have to do this every day."

Mastery in writing, as in every aspect of life, requires a daily commitment, a grounding in craft, experience, and knowledge of the field. Just like any other profession.

Can you imagine going up to a somebody at a party and saying, "You're a physicist? I've been thinking of doing some physics one day"? Or, "You're a heart surgeon? I've been fooling around with the idea of cutting and suturing on the weekend."?

Ought to make for an interesting conversation. At the very least, I bet you won't have to hear about his or her plans to do some writing "one of these days."

Agents

Nothing's more real in the real world of a writer than dealing with agents. However, whenever I'm asked to say something about agents, I feel uneasy. Not because I don't have strong opinions about them, having had varied experiences, good and bad, with agents over a twenty-year span. What makes any discussion of agents so difficult is that, in my view, the most important aspects of a writer's relationship with his or her agent have almost nothing to do with the agent and everything to do with the writer.

Let's face it. If there's a relationship that's as shrouded in mythology, half-truths, and just plain misconceptions as that between agent and client, I've never heard of one. Who's read A. Scott Berg's biography of Maxwell Perkins without thinking, "Jeez, I wish I had an agent like *him.*" That is, until you read about some of the deals legendary agent Swifty Lazar got for *his* clients.

On the down side, we all know horror stories about agents abandoning clients, misrepresenting them, assailing their work, diminishing their esteem. Even the best agents blow hot and cold with their writers, or get distracted by the excitement of snagging a new, *wunderkind* client.

So, before talking about what the writer needs to recognize as his or her own contribution to the sometimes puzzling, often painful relationship between writer and agent, let's list some sobering facts:

1. Your agent is not your parent. It's not the agent's job to encourage, support, or validate your creative ambitions, *insofar as they reflect your inner need to be loved and cherished.* Such needs were your birthright, and hopefully were given to you during your childhood. If, however, they were not, it's not an agent's job to pick up the slack.

2. Your agent is in business to make money. This is not a crime against humanity, an affront to the arts, or a personal repudiation of your aesthetic dreams. It is just a fact.

3. While your agent may indeed admire your talent and share with you lofty creative and financial goals, he or she is not inclined or obligated to care about them as much as you do. In fact, *no one* cares about your career as much as you do. Which means the burden of worrying about your artistic aspirations, income, reputation in the field, and level of personal and professional satisfaction rests entirely on your shoulders.

These three points aside, what every writer needs to understand is that the very nature of the artist's position in society contributes to the asymmetry of the relationship between writer and agent. The moment a writer offers his or her work for evaluation to the marketplace—whether to a book publisher, a magazine editor, a film producer, or a TV network—that writer is instantly placed in the vulnerable position analogous to that of child to caregiver. Since the marketplace holds the power to validate one's work, it retains the ability to mirror back to the writer either affirming or shaming messages about the writer's worth.

When dealing with an agent—a person equally embedded in the machinery of the marketplace—the writer's vulnerabilities encourage him or her either to exaggerate or minimize the agent's opinion; to place an unrealistic burden on the relationship with an agent, in terms of its providing solace and support; and to use, as a child does, the agent's responses as a mechanism for emotional self-regulation.

The reality is, this primarily fiduciary arrangement can't tolerate such burdens. The writer expects too much in the way of esteem building, validation, and empathy. Like those who claim to be looking for a "soul mate" in their romantic relationships—which often betrays a desire for an exact mirror image of oneself so as to minimize conflicts—a writer who searches ardently for an agent who really "gets" him or her at a profound level is doomed to disappointment.

Which means that every unreturned phone call by the agent, every less-than-ecstatic response to a new piece of work, every real or imagined shift in vocal tonality during a conversation are experienced by the writer as concrete indicators of one's self-worth. The wise writer understands this, if only theoretically, and should at least strive to keep his or her relationship with an agent in context. Maybe it will lessen the blows, whatever they are and whenever they come. Then again, maybe it won't.

On the other hand, unlike one's parents, if you don't like your agent, you can always try another one. You'll probably discover that each new agent is just different from, not better than, the last. And that, when it comes to agents, soul mates are few and far between.

Which is good, because then you can get back to your writing, the one true source of any success—financial or otherwise—you're likely to enjoy.

Home of the Heart

It's a famous "Golden Age" Hollywood story. Novelist William Faulkner was working at a film studio on a screenplay and having a hard time with it. Frustrated, he asked the studio executive if he could work on it at home. The exec, desperate to get the thing moving, quickly agreed.

A week later, having heard nothing from Faulkner, the exec called the writer's rented place here in town. But Faulkner wasn't there—when he'd said he wanted to write at home, he meant Mississippi, which is where the studio finally caught up with him.

True or not, the story illustrates something that I've come to see as a crucial element of a writer's life. The idea of home—not necessarily your birthplace, or where you live now, or even a physical location at all. I'm talking about a quality of being "at home" in your surroundings—by which I mean your emotional as well as physical environment.

Take your physical surroundings—where you live. Tennessee Williams once remarked that your birthplace, the town or family or geographical location in which you were raised, was not really your home. When he went to Key West, he said he'd finally found his "home of the heart"—the place whose people, scenery, and ambience reflected more truly who he really was.

My own writer clients speak of this phenomenon all the time. They extol the emotionally restorative, authentic sense of belonging that various places instill. Some find this home in nature, in hikes on forested trails; some on the water, sailing or rowing. Others find it in the familiar bustle of a New York deli.

Particularly for my clients from the East Coast—as so many California writers are—the sense of home is connected to busy streets, a change of seasons, the bracing energy of crowded neighborhoods.

Still others, from small towns, miss the sense of community, of interconnectedness, which paradoxically enables them to endure, and even relish, the solitary experience of writing. The balance of these two extremes, the community of others and the solitude for writing, is where home lies for them.

So, yes, I feel it's important for writers to discover and try to recapture whatever environmental elements feel like home. If nature resuscitates your spirit, then whenever possible go out and find a trail. If community sustains your soul, to the best of your ability create some aspect of this in your life: Join (or form) a writers' group, take a class, get to know your neighbors. If nothing feels more like home than a corned beef on rye, go to your local deli. Whatever.

On the other hand, I'd like you to consider the idea of home in more personal, psychological terms, the concept of a "home of the heart" that starts from within, from an awareness and appreciation of your authentic self—in other words, the notion of being at home in your own skin.

For most of us, arriving at *that* destination is a much harder journey. In fact, it's not a journey at all, but a process. Being at home in your own skin implies an understanding and acceptance of the full range of your thoughts and feelings, a sense of being okay with yourself—not in some sort of New Age conceptualization of bliss—but rather okay with the myriad emotional states that inhabit you, and that you in turn inhabit.

When you can coexist with the thoughts and feelings within you, and find some equanimity in their frequent painfulness and contradiction, then you are truly at home in your own skin.

Of course, *this* "home of the heart" is harder to discover, and the upkeep is considerably more difficult to sustain than the payments on that longed-for mountain cabin or sailboat. The upkeep here is a requirement to stay conscious—to live in a state of wakefulness to your interior life, and to maintain the will to allow all that's inside you to flourish.

Being at home with yourself in this way is crucial if you're to have access to the creativity that's in you, because it's forged from an authentic engagement with all that you are.

It occurs to me, as I end this, that the most famous quote about home is a pretty sobering one: Thomas Wolfe said, "You can't go home again." This may be true, from the standpoint of returning to the past and reexperiencing what you thought and hoped for and believed in.

But when I talk about home, I'm not referring to the past.

165

I'm talking about coming home to yourself, an authentic sense of who you are, moment to moment—the "home of the heart" that's alive in each one of us, only waiting for our creative gift to give it expression.

The Unknown

After almost twelve years as a psychotherapist, the one thing I know for sure is that I don't know anything for sure.

Maybe it's the result of seeing hundreds of clients over the course of my practice, encountering such a wide variety of people, issues, and experiences. Maybe it's the hard-won acceptance of the idea that few things are black or white, true or not true, but rather some mixture of the two. Maybe it's just that I'm getting older.

I was thinking of this the other day, while serving on the panel at a local writing conference. I was seated between a talented, successful screenwriter and an equally talented, successful TV writer. (Since the topic of the panel was "Staying Sane in Show Business," I guess they figured having a therapist aboard wasn't a bad idea.) The audience was made up of sincere, passionately attentive people who seemed to be yearning for something from those of us on the panel. Some answer. Some blueprint for success. Something we knew for sure.

What struggling writer *doesn't* yearn for this? I know I did (and frequently still do). I've taught countless writing workshops over the years and was always moved by questions like "What color paper do you write on?" "Is it better to write in the morning or evening?" "Should a writer always outline first?"

In other words, what did I know (and when did I know it)? And the funny thing is, I used to try to answer those questions, as ultimately unanswerable as they are. I could understand from personal experience the yearning behind them, the struggle to find a path in the dense forest, or at least to identify some markers.

Not that there aren't things to teach, and for writers to learn. Things having to do with craft, consistency, persistence. Things that we all need to learn and relearn, one long unceasing lesson that lasts as many days as we do.

But the most important lesson, the one truth that experienced writers know, is that there's a limit to knowing. Which means there's a limit to safety, sureness, technique. That, regardless of the tools you forge, the gifts you were given at birth, the teachers you meet along the way, sooner or later you bump up against the mystery, the thing that can't be known.

Good writing is a combination of all the aforementioned factors, and yet it transcends all of them. Good writing is bigger than the sum of its parts. You can do everything "right," approach the work with talent, diligence, and craft—and yet, while on Monday the writing will sing, on Tuesday it sinks.

Why? I don't know. More important, you don't have to know. You just have to keep writing.

St. John of the Cross, describing mystical union with the

Almighty, said, "I came into the unknown, beyond all science." Which may be well and good when it comes to mystical unions, but what does that have to do with making your characters richer or solving your Act Two problems?

More than you might think. Regardless of talent level or career success, every writer "comes into the unknown" the moment he or she begins to write. It's part of the compact made between the writer and that which is being written. A compact that reads something like this: "I [the writer] bring to this work my talent, craft, and professionalism; I also bring a fair amount of life experience, emotional baggage, grandiose fantasies, and chaotic dreads; I'm also throwing in some pragmatic understanding of the marketplace, story beats suggested by my agent, character nuances from my writing group, and a couple jokes I'm stealing from that last script nobody bought; finally, I offer my blood, sweat, and tears, enough goodwill to float a hospital ship, and a vague sense of wanting my authentic voice, whatever it may be, to shine through the material."

And what can the writer expect from the other party to this compact—the Muse, the Unknown, whatever name you want to give it? Not much. In fact, expect nothing at all. Except the occasional miracle. The great line of dialogue. The surprising story turn. Those infrequent moments when you look at something you've just written, something wonderful, and say to yourself, "Where the hell did *that* come from?" And your heart soars.

Talk about a risky business! You pour all this talent, energy, and commitment into writing, and there's still no guarantee that anything good will come of it. And when it does, most of the time you won't know why it does.

As I said earlier, good writing is damn mysterious, as much to the writer as anyone else, which is probably the source of its power to move, enthrall, and inspire.

I say "probably," of course, because when it comes to writing, you never know.

Lately, I Don't Like
the Things I Love

Years ago, I worked with a screenwriter client who regularly claimed to have two great loves: her teenaged daughter Susie and writing. I remember vividly her struggles during a particularly turbulent period in her life. Her last two scripts had been shelved by the studio, and a current one had just been handed over to another, younger—and, by implication, "hotter"—writer. On the home front, there were daily battles with her increasingly rebellious daughter. Finally, during one of our sessions, my client came to a painful realization. "Lately," she said haltingly, as though baffled by the idea, "I don't think I like the things that I love."

On the evidence, it was easy to see her dilemma. Now in her forties, she'd worked hard to carve out a screenwriting career. There'd been moderate success, a produced credit or two, with the accompanying money. There'd always been another development deal, a six-week rewrite; her agent always returned her phone calls. But more important than any of these, she'd always loved to write.

But in recent years, things had slowly unraveled. Whether due to ageism or a changing market, her career had stalled. Maybe her own creative energies had flagged: Divorce and a new life as a single parent can do that to you. For whatever reason, the job offers were fewer; her work was more often rejected, or hugely rewritten. She sank into that emotional state so tellingly phrased by Sartre: incomprehension and rage.

Her daughter Susie, now sixteen, was an equally infuriating challenge to the idea of unconditional love. Her rebellion—what therapists blithely refer to as a "period of differentiation"—was taking the usual form: sex, drugs, and an almost pathological inability to agree with her mother about anything.

As we worked together during this period, I kept replaying my client's words in my mind. *Lately, I don't think I like the things that I love.* On the surface, the meaning was clear: She loved her daughter, and she loved writing, but at the moment both seemed to offer nothing but grief, rejection, and humiliation.

But beyond the obvious, what was my client saying to me? That she could only love something as long as she liked it, in the sense of receiving appropriate personal and professional rewards from it? Hardly. Raising her daughter had always been a struggle, as it is for most parents, yet her love for Susie only grew with the years. Likewise her writing career, marked by the same triumphs and failures as most writers experience. Yet she approached every new writing job with the breathless excitement of an astronaut setting foot on a new planet.

So what was I missing? I found out soon enough, during a session, when I reminded her of what she'd said about not liking the things she loved. Apparently, she'd forgotten she'd even said it. She was even embarrassed by it now.

"I said I didn't like Susie? Or writing?"

I nodded. "Not that anyone would blame you. Remember what's been going on with your daughter? As of last week, you two weren't even speaking."

"That's right. I got tired of being told to go screw myself every two minutes."

"As for your career," I continued, "aren't you being re-written by some smart-ass kid who just signed a multimillion-dollar deal with Paramount?"

"Yeah, and thanks for reminding me about his deal. I'd almost succeeded in blocking it out."

"Look," I said, "you're getting hammered by the two things you love most. How *could* you be okay with that?"

"But it has to be okay," she replied. "Or else—"

She paused. I took a guess. "Or else it means you don't *really* love your daughter, and you don't *really* love writing. There's no space in your conception of loving these two things for you to be disappointed. For them to occasionally break your heart."

She nodded. "I'm only allowed to be disappointed in myself . . . for failing them."

I tried to choose my next words carefully. "When we love something, whether our work, a mate, or a child, we'd better figure on disappointing it . . . and enduring the times it will disappoint us. If we're not vulnerable to that, I don't think we have a right to even call it love."

She looked up sharply. Pointed a painted nail in my direction. "Now *you're* starting to piss me off."

"Of course. We're in a relationship, a microversion of the one you have with your daughter, or even with your work. We're bound to piss each other off sometimes."

She sat back in her chair, digesting this. "So I just get through all this . . . this *anger* at everything, until—"

"Until you're okay with it. And then it's just another feeling, more—"

She held up her hand. "I know. More grist for the mill. Christ, you've said it enough times. But the way I've been feeling lately . . . it just sucks."

"Sounds like it."

She looked off, through the picture window. "Getting through this . . . could take a long time."

"Probably. Your relationship to Susie, and to your writing, might go through a lot of changes. But I'm betting you'll come to some sort of peace with both of them."

She gave me a frank look. "A *long* time . . ."

I shrugged. "You going anywhere?"

She hesitated only a moment, then almost smiled. Then shook her head.

Ageism

One of the career issues mentioned in the preceding chapter was my client's battle with ageism. In her forties, she was beginning to feel devalued, and almost unemployable as a screenwriter.

God knows, it's an issue that presents itself constantly in my practice, among not only the clients who have been stigmatized or underemployed because of it, but even among those younger clients who fear it as something that looms further down the line. Ageism, it seems, has joined death and taxes as an inevitability of contemporary life, particularly in the arts. (Though it has spread, like a contagion, to most other careers as well: business, law, advertising, technology.)

The problem with complaining about ageism is that, like the weather, complaining about it and doing something about it are two different things. Everybody knows, at a kind of gut level, that the marketplace's preoccupation with youth is ridiculous. Even a cursory look at who spends how much, on what, and where, indicates that catering solely to the young as consumers is financially shortsighted, artistically bankrupt, and morally suspect.

But aside from marketplace concerns, the really insidious aspect of ageism is that it's based on certain "givens" that rarely hold up under examination. Youth implies a more imaginative, more subversive, less rule-bound approach to creative work. Yet the facts say otherwise. Most young (or new) artists are often quite conservative, retro, and derivative. The way an artist learns craft is by apprenticeship, by using earlier artists as models. We read Hemingway, so our first efforts are almost inevitably Hemingway-ish. We admire Hitchcock, so our early films are filled with Hitchcockian references.

It's my belief that the more mature, confident, and self-trusting an artist is, the more likely he or she is to break with convention, to explore more deeply the difficult and idiosyncratic material of narrative and story. A brief overview of history's most accomplished artists reveals that the majority of their best work was done during their middle-age years.

That said, what can we do, as artists, about the reality of ageism in the current market atmosphere? My guess is, not much, at least in terms of affecting the way the powers-that-be operate. The science of demographics rules the media, and as long as advertisers believe they're reaching their target audience, things will probably stay the way they are.

Do I wish things were different? Sure. But, as I noted earlier, Stephen Levine reminds us, "Suffering is caused by wanting things to be otherwise."

Do I yearn for a return to a simpler time, when creative artists weren't judged by how much hair (and how few wrinkles) they had, but instead by the depth and relevance of their work? You bet. But, as novelist John Fowles reminds us, "All pasts are like poems. You can derive a thousand things, but you can't live in them."

Am I outraged and disgusted that studios, networks, and publishers cravenly pander to what they think the young consumer wants, abdicating their responsibility to develop and promote writing that takes advantage of a wide range of talents, ages, and points of view and ignoring the incontrovertible fact that good stories, well told, appeal to a cross section of audience types? Yes, I am. But as author and psychiatrist Thomas Szasz reminds us, "You can't build a big business on truth."

The point is, we're all getting older. Whether or not, as people and as writers, we accept and address that fact in creative, meaningful, and life-enhancing ways is up to us. Each of us. In other words, how we deal with the fact of ageism, like the fact of aging itself, is an individual choice. A writer can bitch and moan about it, wax nostalgic about the old days, burn with envy every time some hot new writer comes on the scene—or, he or she can accept the rules of the game, the context in which his or her career is inextricably bound, and write. Truly. About the issues, people, events that inspire that writer. Maybe the marketplace will respond. As often as not, it won't.

Or the writer will be asked to modify the material. Make the characters younger, more hip, more relatable to the target audience. Should the artist make these changes? As always, it's a personal choice. If the mortgage is on the line, probably. If not . . . well, then, hopefully not.

Face it, there's no cure for ageism. Like most other "isms" that plague modern society, it probably can't be legislated away. It's a fact of life.

And, as I've often said to my clients, "There is no cure

for life. It's not a problem to be solved. It's an experience to be had, a set of circumstances to be endured, events to be survived, realities to be accepted—more or less on a daily basis, with courage, conviction, humor, and a modicum of hope."

Better than that, nobody can do. No matter how old—or young—they are.

Part Seven

HANGING ON

It is not your obligation to complete your
work, but you are not at liberty to quit.
—THE TALMUD

Ｈow do you work?" someone once asked Einstein.

"I grope," he replied.

That exchange, as far as I'm concerned, is all the instruction a writer needs. It's the sum total of every life lesson he or she could ever hope to learn, the equivalent of a Ph.D. in Being a Writer.

Not an attractive word, *grope*. Sounds too much like *lope*, or *dope*, or *mope*. As an image, groping has associations with unpleasant activities like stumbling around, feeling blindly with your fingers in the dark, or enduring a series of false starts and wrong turns. In other words, as an image it so perfectly captures the experience of writing that most writers I know would dismiss it out of hand as applying to them. It sounds unprofessional, almost haphazard, and too susceptible to the whims of luck and circumstance.

In fact, some might claim, real writers don't grope. They

181

reflect, ponder, conceptualize, synthesize, outline, revise, embellish . . . create. Their writing is the result of craft, inspiration, thought, insight, a deep understanding of character and narrative, and a visceral connection to that which moves and entertains the reader or audience.

To be blunt, a real writer, a pro, knows what the hell he or she is doing! That's why it's a profession, not a hobby. That's why most people can't do it.

And I agree. Up to a point.

Make no mistake, I differentiate between professional writers and would-be, Sunday-afternoon, all-talk-and-no-pages amateurs. If anything, I've emphasized many times in this book the virtues of craft, experience, and consistent labor as the bedrock requirements for a productive, successful writing life.

But I'm talking about something else here. I'm suggesting that a professional writer's view of his or her work include in it the reality that all artistic effort, in the final analysis, is a groping toward something. Makes no difference whether it be a story point, a character nuance, or a thematic idea. Hell, even if you're just groping toward a better, funnier joke. A true professional, a real craftsperson, knows that the tools of creative preparation—story construction, careful reflection on theme and content, an understanding of character based on observing how real people (including oneself) behave—these tools have been developed for one reason only: to enable the artist to grope, hopefully with confidence and self-trust, perhaps with fear and self-doubt, but nonetheless to grope toward something, some way of expressing an idea, some way to evoke a chill, a tear, a laugh, a nod of recognition.

Just as a seasoned writer acknowledges and includes all

of his or her feelings in a piece of writing, granting doubt and fear equal validity with faith and courage, so too does that seasoned writer understand that past a certain point, a true artist gropes. In a way, it's only logical. The higher your level of professionalism, the more likely you are to break away from the known ways of doing things. Grounded in craft and experience, true artists invariably move beyond the bounds of conventional thought and approaches. Which means, finally, pushing into new, uncharted territory, the creative unknown . . . where the artist is likely to discover that, regardless of his or her discomfort, groping is the only game in town.

It's a real paradox, when you think about it: It's only when you reach a high level of competence, forged by time and discipline and experience, that you're finally able to grope. Of course, at such a level, things get harder, not easier; you find that you're demanding even more of yourself.

Again, an anecdote from Einstein's life: When a student complained about his difficulties in math, Einstein replied, "Don't worry about your troubles with mathematics. I can assure you mine are far worse."

(In case you're wondering, I'm using examples from Einstein's career for a reason. I figure if I can convince you that a mind of *his* caliber was sanguine about the notion of groping, maybe minds like yours and mine can get on board with the idea, too.)

It's a challenging concept, I admit—that when all is said and done, the best an artist can do is grope. It's about as irritating as accepting that we can't really control things, or that true progress comes from risk, or that, as William Goldman reminds us, nobody knows anything.

On the other hand, it makes a kind of sense. Each of us

is groping, on a daily basis, in our lives, our work, our relationships. The more we learn, the less we seem to know. So we grope toward some understanding, some sense of meaning.

Why should writing, that which best holds the mirror up to ourselves, do any more . . . or less?

Commitment

As a therapist, one of the themes that emerges often in my work with clients is commitment. In dealing with relationship issues, for example, the depth of a commitment is tested by fears about the future, questions about trust and fidelity, and concerns about the tension between dependence and independence.

Likewise, clients with children struggle daily with the commitment to the rigors of parenthood—the emotional and financial responsibilities, the sharp changes in lifestyle, the balancing of one's needs with those of one's child.

For my writer clients, this same level of commitment is required. It's the key to hanging on in the face of the rejection, fatigue, and feelings of inadequacy a writing career can often foster and reinforce.

Further, I believe the relationship a writer has with his or her writing is analogous to that of any committed relationship, with the same joys and pains, pleasures and demands.

And, likewise in all relationships, a commitment to writing needs to be nurtured, tended.

What does a commitment to your writing entail? The same things as a commitment to a mate, a partner, or a child. The following come to mind:

Constancy. You've got to be in it for the long haul. You're not going anywhere. You'll be at the typewriter or computer screen tomorrow, and the day after that, and the day after that.

Resilience. Things aren't always going to go well. There'll be good writing days and bad ones, great pages and awful ones. The test of any committed relationship is your willingness to accept (and endure) the disappointments as well as the triumphs. A commitment to the writing life has the same requirement.

Fluidity. "The best laid plans," etc., etc. If something isn't working, you try something else. A long-term commitment requires the ability to learn from mistakes and to give up cherished notions about the way things "should" be. So too a writer committed to his or her craft is both its student and master, learning from wrong turns and stale ideas, trying new approaches, coaxing the work along and following where it leads. This keeps the writing fresh, alive, even dangerous sometimes. Which, for a writer, is both exciting and nervewracking. (The parallels to marriage and parenting are self-evident!)

Openness to surprise. A corollary to fluidity, this aspect of a real commitment to writing challenges us to be open to a surprising twist of story, or an unexpected nuance of a character we thought we knew. It's welcoming a dark or comic spin that seems to come to us like a devil's whisper, urging us to pursue it.

An openness to surprise reminds us why we made the commitment in the first place—because the task of writing, of creating something from nothing, acts upon *us* as much as we upon *it,* and the surprise of our own humor, rage, passion, and empathy thrills us, fulfills us. A friend of mine once said, "We write so that we won't die." An openness to surprise keeps our commitment to writing alive.

Patience. As I've argued, true patience is simply the act of waiting, with or even without expectation, for the next moment to arrive. Hopeful, watchful, it's the testing of faith in ourselves and that to which we're committed. A trait as valuable as a good work ethic, a writer's patience is aided by curiosity about what's coming next and a conviction that it will probably be worth the wait.

In my view, the real test of a writer's commitment is that he or she would rather be there, waiting, working, fretting, than anywhere else.

Love. Love is the foundation of commitment: Having the faith, endurance, or just plain stubbornness to stay committed against all odds is meaningless without love. A writer who doesn't love writing can't make a real commitment to it—instead, all the struggles, the highs and lows, become merely a test of one's will, or ego.

Without love, one can perhaps survive the writer's life—maybe even garner some success in the marketplace—but what you're committed to lies elsewhere. Without love, the true joy of writing—that mysterious kinship with what you write, that transcendence of yourself whenever what you've written has literally captured your heart—is rarely felt.

A commitment to writing, in the end, means that you accept, with as much grace as you can muster on any given day, its myriad demands and delights, failures, and triumphs.

Of course, like in any committed relationship, sometimes it seems like *you're* doing all the giving. But then, when you least expect it, it gives something back, and you remember again why you love it, its meaning in your life.

And, over and above this, you have the sublime experience of allegiance to something other than, and perhaps greater than, yourself.

News Flash: Writing Is Hard!

The legendary screenwriter Ben Hecht once said something very profound about how hard any kind of writing is: "It takes just as much effort to make a toilet seat as it does a castle window; only the view is different."

I think about this quote sometimes when clients express concern about the quality of the project they're currently writing for. Especially during Oscar season, when the best screenplay awards are in contention. Or when the National Book Award winners are announced. Or when the Lannan Foundation awards its annual grants. "What am I doing writing *this* crap," a typical client laments, "when Frank McCourt comes out with *Angela's Ashes?*"

If my client and I investigate this further, what often emerges is the fear that, if actually given the opportunity, he or she wouldn't be up to doing the job.

One of my screenwriter clients, who makes a handsome income writing big studio thrillers, admitted this very concern to me recently. "Hell, I have a hard enough time writing *this* stuff. What makes me think I could even come close to turning out a *Chinatown* or *Lawrence of Arabia* or *Some Like It Hot?*"

The mistake this client makes—and one shared by many writers—is the notion that doing a good job on elevated types of material is *necessarily* harder than writing a paperback suspense novel or funny sitcom episode. What makes *Angela's Ashes* a great book is the author's courage in exploring his own family's history and his passion to tell that story. What makes Robert Towne's *Chinatown* a classic script is the level of craft, intelligence, and sophistication brought to it. These same qualities, to whatever extent the writer possesses them, are what should be brought to *any* kind of writing, regardless of medium or genre. If approached in this spirit, the writer is doing his or her best to make the material work, whatever the material.

Which is what makes writing so damned hard. To do anything at a high level of competence—whether writing a novel, being in a relationship, or building a canoe—is difficult because it requires those aforementioned qualities of craft, passion, and intelligence. If we believe that what we're doing is unworthy of our exerting these qualities, it only makes the task harder.

One way to deal with this attitude is to remember that the writing of *anything* presents us with the opportunity to explore ourselves, to mine our feelings and personal experiences to give the material relevance for us—and our readers or audience. (Hell, it usually happens anyway, outside of our conscious awareness. Years ago, as a novice staff writer on *Welcome Back, Kotter,* I was often creating situations for the characters that mirrored things that had happened to me, or else were yearned-for events and outcomes that resonated from my own personal history. At the time, of course, I was totally oblivious to such connections. But the supportive, humorous things that Gabe Kotter often said to a particular Sweathog in a moment of crisis invariably reflected the kind of interaction I'd wished for as a child.)

The point is, whether or not you're writing a project whose artistic goals are as lofty as your own, you've been given an opportunity to express yourself through your talent. To do this at its highest level, to bring the best of yourself to the project, will paradoxically mean that it's going to be hard work.

Maybe even as hard as writing an Academy Award–winning script or a Pulitzer Prize–winning series of news-paper articles. Because all good writing demands the same elements of pacing, characterization, story beats, set-up, and pay-off. All good writing requires you to sweat blood over the narrative, the getting of a character from Point *A* to Point *B* in a way that makes sense, even if only in terms of the internal logic of the material you're given.

And make no mistake: Every type of genre, in every media, no matter how apparently low-brow the artistic aims, has it own internal logic. From a Hallmark card to a *Hallmark Hall of Fame*, from a romance novel to the umpteenth sequel to *Die Hard*, every narrative requires an internal logic for it to connect to its audience.

Another point to consider: You, the writer, can view each writing assignment as an opportunity to learn, to stretch your talent, to try something different. In my own Holly-wood career, which ranged from writing jokes for stand-up comics to sitcoms to feature films, I learned something new

191

from every assignment. I also learned about my own resiliency, willingness to grow, and resistance to growth. Every new script was a life lesson.

Yes, writing is hard. Writing *anything* is hard. Especially if you're doing your best.

Which reminds me of another favorite Hollywood story. Years ago, a roomful of studio writers were going crazy trying to beat an Act Two problem in a script they were doing. After almost a week of teeth gnashing and garment rending, a new, young writer was brought into the room. In a matter of minutes, he hit upon the solution. To which one of the exhausted old veterans grumbled, "*Sure* he beat it. He didn't know how hard it was."

Burnout: A Modest Proposal

It was a dark and stormy night—

Well, actually it wasn't, but it should've been. It was somewhere near 2 A.M., and I was stuck in the second act of my third draft of a screenplay I was growing to hate.

Getting out the second draft had been hard enough, given all the changes dictated by a studio executive who gave new meaning to the term *unqualified*. This in addition to being continually undermined at meetings by the producer, who responded to any criticisms of the script by turning to me and saying, "See, kid? I *told* ya it wouldn't work."

Anyway, I'd gotten halfway through my third pass at the script when the phone rang. It was a Monday morning, and my producer had just spent the weekend back East in his hometown, at his high school's twentieth reunion.

"Kid," he said, "I got a great idea. Our hero's gotta go back to his high school reunion."

"Huh?" I said, or words to that effect.

"*Billy,* the cop," he said excitedly. "He goes back to his

twentieth reunion . . . maybe he meets his old girlfriend, maybe he screws her, I don't know."

"His high school reunion? I mean, why should we do that? What does that have to do with—"

"C'mon, it's character stuff. Shows another side of the guy. 'Road not taken,' that kinda shit . . ."

"But . . . but . . ."

No amount of debate, badgering, or pleading could convince him that a plot-shattering, logic-bending detour to a high school reunion wasn't just the thing our story needed. After I hung up the phone, I consoled myself with the thought that it could've been worse: He might've had a UFO encounter that weekend, which would've *really* screwed up the script.

Which brings me back to that dark and stormy night (though it was actually moonlit and balmy). Two in the morning, and I'm standing in my office, looking out at the trees and the silent houses, and I'm thinking about how everybody else on the block is sleeping peacefully in their beds, or else making love, or watching an all-night *Twilight Zone* marathon, or even breaking into an appliance store down on Ventura Boulevard—doing *anything else* but trying to shoe-horn a damned high school reunion into a story that it doesn't belong in.

In short, it occurs to me that everybody in L.A. is having a better time than I am!

The preceding drama happened many years ago, when I was a callow young screenwriter, but I think of that night often, especially when my writer clients complain of similar mind-numbing, jaw-dropping, heart-clutching experiences.

By that, I don't mean the struggles with the movie studios, book publishers, magazine editors, and agents that make up the daily life of a writer. I'm talking about something else, torments that go way deeper, that carve you up and empty you out. Those umpteenth-draft, Dark Night of the Soul, "there's-gotta-be-a-better-way-to-earn-a-living-than-this" feelings.

In other words, burnout.

Let's face it, being a writer is an unusual profession. It floats somewhere on the continuum between a calling and a curse. It shares with the other art forms a kind of fringe, marginalized position in society. It tends to embarrass family and friends. Other professions look upon it with skepticism, if not downright suspicion.

Writing can also be a lonely, isolating experience, broken up occasionally by encounters with other writers who've invariably just signed lucrative network development deals or three-book publishing contracts.

No wonder that, on occasion, a writer can feel like the Poster Child for depression, loss of energy, and stress. I don't have a client in my practice who hasn't felt "fried" sometimes, burned out.

Like any other creative impulse, the urge to write is born of experiences, thoughts, and emotional responses to the world around you. Even if writing is merely a business to you, a way to earn money, it still requires raw materials. When you're burned out, these emotional, intellectual, and aesthetic resources are unavailable to you.

My advice for treating writer's burnout is simple: Let yourself burn out. Really.

Mark Twain knew how (and when) to rest and take the necessary time to recharge his creative batteries. He referred to it as "waiting for the well to fill up again."

In the same way, you might try thinking of burnout as

an integral part of the writing process, as important to your productive output as it is for a farmer who lets his crops go unplanted for a season. He knows the soil needs to replenish itself to stay fertile. In the same manner, if you don't panic, acknowledging and accepting feelings of burnout can be equally restorative.

Because, frankly, if writing *is* your life, that "well" will inevitably refill, and once again you'll be back in the game.

Even when that game involves sending a cop back to his high school reunion in the middle of a manhunt for a serial killer.

But I'm not bitter.

A Writer's Library

I've been quoting from my favorite writing books throughout this book, valuing the clarity and wisdom of the many
writers who've struggled with some of the same concerns
I've raised. I think it's a good idea to read about writing for
a number of reasons—mostly having to do with the development of craft—but primarily because it helps to alleviate
the sense of isolation that can accompany writing. The
question is, which books?

Everyone knows the better-selling ones, and I can certainly recommend them without reservation: *Writing Down
the Bones* and *Wild Mind* by Natalie Goldberg, Anne Lamott's
Bird by Bird, Julia Cameron's *The Artist's Way*. And, for the
mythological underpinnings of narrative, Joseph Campbell's
justly famous *Hero with a Thousand Faces*.

I'm also a big fan of William Goldman's book about movie
writing, *Adventures in the Screen Trade*. (I once mentioned

it glowingly to a studio executive I knew, who exclaimed, "I *hate* that book!"—a ringing endorsement if I've ever heard one.)

However, I'd like to suggest some other books, personal favorites, that I think speak more powerfully and tellingly to the inner life of the writer. Not only are they wonderfully soul satisfying, but they address the core of the creative experience. Not how-to books (or even how-to-survive), they're more concerned with how to *be*. Though not all these books are about writing specifically, the issues explored are relevant to anyone living the writer's life.

In Praise of What Persists, edited by Stephen Berg. A collection of essays by a variety of writers detailing the personal experiences that influenced their work.

Zen and the Art of Motorcycle Maintenance, by Robert Pirsig. A great book on the dynamic—and often crazy-making—process of striving for quality, however you define it.

The Writing Life, by Annie Dillard. Elegant and personal, as well as hard-nosed and pragmatic. Wonderful reading.

The Illusion of Technique, by William Barrett. A book I'm always pressing on friends and colleagues. A ringing defense of creativity as a spontaneous and powerful reaction against the false sense of security promised by reliance on rigid structures and techniques.

Life Work, by Donald Hall. A beautifully written book by the much-honored poet and man of letters, exploring his obsession with—and consolation from—a life devoted to the craft of writing.

Mastery, by George Leonard. Mentioned earlier, it's a primer on the value of practice, the consistent *doing* of a craft. A strong rebuttal to a goal-oriented approach to creativity—and to life.

The Courage to Create, by Rollo May. The title says it all.

On Moral Fiction, by John Gardner. Densely written, frankly pedantic, and inevitably self-righteous—and those arc the things I *like* about it. A stirring, somctimcs maddening call-to-arms on behalf of writers taking what they do—and its effects on society—seriously.

The Journals of Eugene Delacroix. I know what you're thinking: "What do the personal journals of a French painter, written a couple hundred years ago, have to say to me, a modern writer?" You'd be surprised. Delacroix's honest, vulnerable self-appraisal, his struggle to balance the pragmatic demands of life with his artistic goals, his emotional swings from elation to despair and back again, are both fascinating in their own right and a timeless reflection of the dilemmas faced by all creative people.

The Great Gatsby, by F. Scott Fitzgerald. Sixty thousand perfect words. A masterpiece of lucidity, banked emotional fire, sustained tone, depth, and heart. I try to read it once a year, just to clear out the cobwebs.

And, finally, a small gem that's spawned a dozen imitators (particularly of variations on its title). I'm referring to *Zen in the Art of Archery,* by Eugen Herrigel. Written with simplicity and humility, it's the one book I'd advise reading if you can't get around to any of the others mentioned previously. For writers—for everyone—this is *the* book. Why? I could list many reasons, but mostly you learn about the importance of . . . breathing. (Trust me on this. Go read this book. Slowly. Savor it. Hopefully, afterward, at a level outside of your conscious awareness, it'll go to work on you.)

There you have it. An eclectic group, I admit. There are other worthy books I could've included, by writers as diverse as E. B. White and Ray Bradbury, Ben Hecht and Stephen King. But for now, I'll stick with my list. Good companions on the writer's journey. Enjoy.

A Stillness That
Characterizes Prayer

Despite its difficulties and challenges, the writing life has much to recommend it—the excitement of creation, the chance to explore our thoughts and emotions, the opportunity to communicate our ideas and experiences to others, etc. But you know one of the things I like best about writing? It's quiet.

I was thinking about this the other day, when I ran across a quote by novelist Saul Bellow. He talked about the act of writing as possessing "a stillness that characterizes prayer." I suspect what he was referring to is the quietude that both accompanies the act of writing and that makes the act of writing possible in the first place. In essence, writing as meditation; quietude in the midst of chaos. Not such a bad thing.

As we begin a new century, certain hard truths are evident. Things in general have become more complex, our lives have gotten busier and more difficult to manage, and a kind of low-level anxiety attends the arrival of each new technological and/or social advance. Plus, as Alvin Toffler warned, in his book *Future Shock,* the pace of all these changes is too rapid to allow us much time to integrate and assimilate their meanings.

The point is, to the person of reasonable intelligence and sensibilities, it can all seem a bit much. Overwhelming. Chaotic. *Noisy.*

When I said that one of the things I like about writing is that it's quiet, I wasn't being facetious. Nor was I conceptualizing the silence of writing as an escape or withdrawal from the world. On the contrary, if done truly and from an authentic connection to our hearts and minds, writing is one of the most engaged acts we can do. It's a way of speaking to oneself, and then to the world, that is as daring an adventure as scaling a mountain or sailing solo across the North Atlantic.

In fact, the writer's quiet I'm talking about doesn't even require actual silence. Writers often listen to music, or write in crowded diners, or talk into tape recorders while jogging on the beach.

No, I'm talking about something else. Quietude. A hushed, private space to which a writer is granted access by the act of writing itself. *This* silence, the silence in which most writers write, is the felt sense of their inner world, their aesthetic, their yearnings. It's like a bubble in which thoughts and feelings can intertwine, take shape and unravel, then form new shapes. Like the meditative act, it's a way to cut out the "noise" and just be with who you are, moment to moment, and observe this without judgment.

Also, as in meditation, the silence of writing allows you

to experience the tension between *being* and *doing*. This tension is the source of all good writing. It could, in fact, be considered a definition of the act of writing itself: the constantly reciprocating interplay between being and doing, between experiencing something and then attempting to put that experience into an artfully crafted shape that can communicate to the reader or audience.

There's another, deeper level to this. In my own experience, the "stillness that characterizes prayer" in this writer's space makes possible the sensation of losing oneself, the ego, the "I" that writes. What emerges is the sense that "it" is writing, some groundless flowing expression of creativity and intent, for which the writer is merely the vehicle.

As one of my clients put it, it's like taking dictation from the movie screen playing in your head. It's the writer's "rush." It's getting out of your own way and letting the writing take over.

There is nothing the least bit "New Age-y" about it. It's as common as stone, and just about as stubbornly resistant to interpretation. If, as I believe, writing is a calling, then the silence that attends the writing act is and should be similar to that of prayer.

And, like prayer, respectful, of both yourself and the writing process. Hopeful, both for yourself and for the product that results from the writing process. And, finally, a waiting, in that hushed, private writer's space, for the conversation to begin between you and your creative self.

Part Eight

DISPATCHES FROM
THE FRONT

Believe those who are seeking the truth;
doubt those who find it.

—ANDRE GIDE

I can't do this anymore," my new client said. He was a TV writer, and this was our first session together.

"Do what?" I asked.

"*This*. Writing. Meetings. Pitching. Hustling my agent. *This!* . . . I can't do it anymore."

I could tell we weren't talking about burnout, or writer's block, or fatigue. Something deeper was stirring.

"It's no life for a grown man," he went on. "I'm gonna be forty soon, for Christ's sake. I got a family that'd like to see their old man once in a while. And when they *do* see me, I'm always moping around, or else pissed off."

"Sure you're not exaggerating?"

"I mean it," he went on. "Those are my two moods—depressed or angry. Except when I'm excited about a script, or things look good after a pitch meeting. *Then* I'm manic, bouncing off the walls, too excited to eat or sleep, and scared shitless the feeling will go away if things fall through."

I nodded. "No question, a writer's life is tough. Not everyone can do it. Perhaps you can muster some appreciation for yourself that you've done this well, survived this long."

"Okay, I'll give myself a medal."

He fell silent for a full minute. I could feel the urgency of what he wanted to say, the sudden need to get it all out.

"Here's the thing," he said finally, words coming sharp and fast. "I get on staff, the show tanks, my agent tries to get me another show. Only it looks like everybody's just hiring their friends. Or the new kid with the hot spec script. So my agent says to me—I mean, I've done three network shows, dozens of episodes—my agent says, 'We need something fresh from you. Why don't you knock out a new spec?' In other words, prove all over again that I know how to write. Why the hell do we put up with it?"

I shrugged. "Depends on your theoretical stance. In behavioral psych terms, it's because of intermittent reinforcement."

"Thanks. I feel a whole lot better now."

"All that means is, being a Hollywood writer is like playing a slot machine in Vegas. You pull the handle down four times, you hit the jackpot. Pull four *more* times and you get zip. You *know* another jackpot's in there, but you don't know how many pulls it'll take to win. So you pull a dozen more. Nothing. You walk away, the next guy comes up, pulls once, and he's got a lap full of silver dollars. *Damn,* you think. If only I'd pulled it *one more time.*"

"So you start lookin' for another slot machine."

"That's right. In experimental tests, the one type of reward system that keeps lab animals trying over and over again is intermittent reinforcement."

He gave a strained little laugh. "So *that's* all we are—

208

hamsters on a treadmill? With the occasional reward of a job to keep us going? . . . No wonder we're miserable."

"Sure . . . if the only rewards you recognize are the ones Hollywood offers. Like I said, it depends on your point of view. As it happens, I don't put much stock in behavioral theories. They're a limited, impoverished view of human beings. Frankly, they don't do us justice."

"They don't?"

"To my way of thinking, good creative work is *itself* the reward. The only one that sustains over the life of a career."

"Hell, I know that intellectually. But it doesn't pay the mortgage, it doesn't get your scripts to bankable stars."

"You're right, it doesn't. It just keeps you sane."

"Big deal. That and four bucks will get you a *café latte*."

I took a few moments to collect my thoughts.

"Look," I said, "if you connect your happiness, your sense of creative meaning, only to those times you sell something, or land a job, or get a script produced, then you're allotting yourself a precious few, isolated moments of fulfillment. Further, you give over totally to others the power to grant you that fulfillment. If you're only going to feel good about your writing at those times, then you're accepting the idea that your worth comes from outside of you, rather than from within."

"Hey, that sounds good, but in the face of all the struggle, the bullshit—I mean, sometimes it's just so hard—"

"I know. You feel you just can't do it anymore."

"I *can't*. I mean, at least, that's what I'm startin' to tell myself." He paused. "Do you think any other writers ever feel that way?"

"Only all of them."

"Yeah, *right*."

"I'm serious." I held his gaze. "You think all the writers I see in here come to therapy because things are going great? That they don't feel frustrated, beaten down, disheartened? Every writer I know has wanted to throw in the towel sometimes. Hell, I'm beginning to think if a writer *doesn't* feel like doing that once in a while, he's just not paying attention."

"Oh." A rueful smile. "Well, that's something . . . But I *still* think writing's a bitch."

"Point taken. In fact, that's a pretty good place for us to pick this up again." I glanced at the table clock. "Same time next week?"

"I'll be here," he said.

"So will I," I said.

Phone Call from Paradise

The preceding session never took place. Like the others in this section, it's an amalgam of hundreds of sessions with clients I've had in my practice. It's also representative of the kinds of issues nearly every writer struggles with.

I think of the preceding vignette, as well as the ones that follow, as dispatches from the writing wars, examples of the different ways writers cope with the pains and joys of the artistic life.

In my view, writers are always the ones on the front lines. They're the creators, the originators, the ones who are the first to say "What if . . . ?" The Oscar-winning film usually starts with the writer's idea, and then everybody else climbs on board (subsequently taking most of the credit). The Nobel Prize–winning novel starts in a room somewhere, a writer alone in a room, with a whole universe of possibility as sole companion. The series of newspaper articles that bring down a powerful city mayor begins with the writer who noticed a discrepancy, sensed a lie, followed his or her creative instincts to the heart of the story.

Henry Miller said it best. "Imagination is the voice of daring. If there is anything God-like about God, it is that. He dared to imagine everything."

But most writers feel decidedly *un*-God-like. Between managing the pragmatic demands of the real world and sorting out the internal conflicts arising from talent and artistic ambition, the daily struggle of the writer's life has the power to dilute the vision and constrict the soul. Often enough, the only thing the writer's imagination can conjure up is all the reasons he or she is going to fail.

That's why so many would-be writers consider giving up the fight, threaten to go AWOL from the front lines. Some even do so.

Others don't. But it's a constant battle, an unending struggle with both the world outside the writer and the world within. And it's anybody's guess, on any given day, which way the decision will go.

For instance, there was another TV writer in my practice who one day left five breathless messages within the space of an hour on my voice mail. What made this so unusual was that he was on vacation in Kauai.

I called him back at the number he'd left, a lone pay phone near a cluster of cottages at some small, exclusive resort. I could hear waves lapping the shore, but I could barely hear *him*. He seemed to be whispering.

"Can you speak up?" I said.

"I said, I'm not coming back."

"To therapy?" This surprised me; I'd thought we'd been making some progress.

"Therapy? No . . . I mean, I'm not coming back to L.A."

"What? And why are you whispering?"

"I gotta keep it down. My wife's in the cottage, but the walls are made outta palm leaves or somethin'. She'll hear me."

"Oh." A therapeutic pause. He bit.

"Look, I don't want her to know. Not yet. In fact, I'm thinking of letting her and the kids go back to L.A. without me. Tell 'em I need a couple extra days on my own to relax, unwind."

"Is this true?"

"Are you kiddin'? I'm co-producer on a sitcom in its second season, with a bad time slot and a flaming psychotic in the lead. What do *you* think?"

"But that's why you're on vacation. Some much-needed R&R. Remote cottage, right on the ocean, no phones or faxes. Sounded great when we talked about it in session."

"It *is* great. That's why I'm not coming back."

"For an extra couple days?"

"For the rest of my *life*, man. But I'm not stayin' *here*. Too civilized. You can still get here by boat, or helicopter."

"I'm not following you."

"Damn right. *Nobody* is. See, once I get Helen and the kids on that plane home, I'm leaving this place and heading for parts unknown. Some little island off New Guinea, or maybe the Hindu Kush. Didja know they got parts there that are still unexplored, that aren't on any map?"

"You're serious."

"Hell, yeah. Look, I'm overweight, overworked, and overstressed. I got a nut the size of your average country, a wife who hates me, two kids who hate *both* of us, an agent, three attorneys, a business manager, a domestic staff that rivals Brideshead, four cars, and a black lab that sees a grooming stylist, a shrink, *and* a pet psychic. With the whole damn thing on my shoulders. That means putting in an eighty-hour workweek, cranking out jokes and story ideas, with the goddamn network breathing down my neck, all while negotiating office politics that would baffle Elizabeth R. Screw it, I'm goin' over the wall."

"Okay, I get how stressed you feel, how trapped—"

"I mean, I'm not even *runnin'* the show. Remember when I told you how I always wanted to create and run a series of my own?"

"Yes, I think I do—"

"Yeah, well, I musta been crazy. You know what being a show-runner's like? Talk about dead men walkin' . . ."

"It *can* be very demanding, and murder on your personal life. But, if you work at it, you can find a balance."

He chuckled, a weary rasp in his whispered voice. "I've been looking for that balance for eighteen years. You know what *I* think? I think it's like net profit points in your contract—some kinda urban myth."

I tried a different approach. "Okay, let's say you just drop out of sight. Live on some uncharted island somewhere. What will you do all day?"

"I was thinking along the lines of drinking and chasing women. And sleeping. Yeah, I could really get into some major sleeping."

"That could get old. What about your mind? Your creativity?"

"What's it done for me lately?"

"Well," I said quietly, clearly stalling for time. I took a breath. "Think about it. It takes imagination to plot an escape from your life. A certain aesthetic daring."

"Yeah, I'm like David Copperfield. One minute I'm here,

the next I'm gone. The Man Who Dropped Out." His voice caught. "Hey . . . wait a minute."

"What?" It was as though I could hear his mind working.

"I was just thinking," he said, "with computers and the Net and satellite tracking, how hard it would be for a guy to really disappear. But finally, after all these close calls, he pulls it off. But then, what if his wife *had* to find him, their daughter needs a kidney transplant or something . . ."

I noticed his voice rising, no longer speaking in a whisper.

"You're not whispering. Won't Helen hear you?"

"Eh?" he answered distractedly. "Nah, she came outta the cottage. I think she went snorkeling or something. But listen—what if the guy's ex-business partner is looking for him, too? Millions are at stake. They hire these mercenaries to find him . . ."

His voice trailed off. All I could hear were those waves lapping again.

"Hello?" I said at last. "You still there?"

"Look," he said quickly, "can we talk about that other stuff when I get back?"

"If you want. But I thought—"

"Maybe I'm losin' it, but this is a *great* freaking idea for a series, 9 o'clock slot. I can work it off that development deal I got at Fox. . . . I mean, I don't know if I ever told you, but I always wanted to run my own show."

"I think I recall you mentioning it."

"Uh-huh. Look, I gotta hang up and make some notes. See ya next week, our regular time?"

"Uh . . . sure." Somewhat at a loss, I added, "Aloha."

But he'd already hung up.

215

The Idea Man

"I don't have a single idea!"

My client, a veteran screenwriter, sat across from me, hands clutching his chair arms. "I've cleared the time, promised my agent a new spec script—"

I shook my head. "And no good ideas?"

"I said, *no ideas, period!* No good ones, bad ones, crazy ones. Zilch! *Nada!*" He tapped his forehead. "It's empty. There's nobody home. I've hit the wall. Pick your metaphor. I'm out of ideas. I can't think of a single thing to write about."

I took a breath. "Look, I know how frustrating that can be. You feel stuck, or unmotivated. But remember, you've been in this place before, and sooner or later . . ."

"This is different," he said impatiently. "And I don't feel stuck. I *do* feel motivated, inspired, whatever the hell you wanna call it. I'm ready, willing and able to dive in on a new project."

Here he seemed to deflate, as he let out a long sigh. "I

216

just can't come up with an idea. Not even a premise, a place to start. Nothing."

A long silence fell between us. In the course of his therapy, one of the themes that had emerged was the painful meaning he gave to any problems with his work. Rather than see his creative struggles as the normal difficulties of the professional writer's life, he felt that "real" writers transcended the kinds of doubts, fears, and blocks to which he regularly succumbed.

The one area where he'd felt secure was as an "idea man"— he often said that though his "pure writing talent" was in question, he could always be confident of the unending supply of story ideas he could come up with.

But now, convinced that he was *out* of ideas? It didn't take a therapist to see what impact this belief would have on him.

"Let's back up a minute," I said. "While I don't think it's likely you've actually run out of ideas, I take seriously your belief that you have. What's important is what that would mean to you."

He practically shot up out of his chair. "It means I'm screwed! My career is over, my family leaves me, and I end up living in a cardboard box."

"Well, as long as you're keeping this in perspective."

"Very funny. Look, I'm not an idiot. I've been a writer for almost twenty years. I know there aren't really any new ideas. Every idea is a variation of some old idea. Some reversal, or switch. It's like moving puzzle pieces around— they're always the same pieces, but if you put 'em together in a new way, the picture's different. Or just different enough."

"And you feel you've suddenly lost this skill?"

"Like I never had it. Gone. I feel like I've been found out, exposed."

"Which means?"

"The jig's up. I oughtta just confess to my wife and kids. Find a rabbi. Hire a psychic. Go underground." A rueful look. "No perspective again, eh?"

I shrugged. "On the contrary, *I'm* convinced. As an idea man, I'd say you're finished."

"Thanks a lot." His face clouded. "So where does that leave me?"

"Defenseless. The last protection you had against really exploring your beliefs about yourself is gone. You don't have being an 'idea man' to hide behind anymore."

His voice grew an edge. "What the hell are you talking about?"

"Writers often hide their insecurities behind an *image* of themselves, some stereotypical description—a 'joke machine,' a 'character guy,' a 'horror writer'—to protect themselves. It *can* be a candid view of a writer's strengths, but it can also be limiting, constrictive, defensive. And, of course, the marketplace reinforces this, putting writers into rigid categories as well."

"Tell me about it."

"The point is, maybe thinking of yourself solely as an 'idea man' has outworn its usefulness for you."

"But if I gave it up, I'd have nothing left to fall back on."

"Which, for a writer, can be either terrifying or liberating. Probably both."

He chewed on this for a moment. "But what do I do now?"

"You might try writing from a different place. Say, starting from character."

"But I don't even *have* a lead character."

"Sure you do. An 'idea man' who thinks he's run out of ideas."

"You mean, a guy like me? But what could happen?"

I made a big show of looking off into space. "Let me see. He could confess to his wife and kids, find a rabbi, hire a psychic. Etcetera."

He smiled. "That sounds vaguely familiar."

"Well, like you said, there are no new ideas. It's just a matter of what you do with them."

"Yeah, yeah," he said, reaching for a pad and pen. "But since it's probably the last good idea I'll ever have, it couldn't hurt to write it down. . . ."

I've Come a Long Way on Paper

Years ago, as part of my internship in psychotherapy, I worked at a private psychiatric facility that specialized in the treatment of patients diagnosed with schizophrenia.

I remember one patient very clearly, a bright, creative young woman in her twenties who suffered terrible, persecutory hallucinations. As a result, she'd spent most of her adolescent and teen years in the mental health system.

Going from institution to institution, her case file had likewise grown over the years. By the time she'd become a patient at our facility, her file was a three-inch stack of treatment notes, progress reports, and evaluations.

One day, she came into group therapy and read a poem she'd written, whose first line, tellingly, was "I've come a long way on paper." The poem was rueful, bitterly self-mocking, frequently hilarious, and ultimately heartbreaking. As was she.

She came to mind recently, while working with a screenwriter client struggling with his lack of success in the business. Despite a half-dozen spec scripts admired by knowledgeable friends and potential buyers in the marketplace, he had yet to sell one, or land a writing assignment. Yet he'd been writing for years. His talent had ripened, his craft had strengthened with each script. He was getting better and better, as the script pages mounted up.

In other words, he'd come a long way as a writer—but only on paper.

"It's like the universe is sending me a message," he said, leaning forlornly against my crowded bookshelf.

"Which is?" I asked.

"'Keep your day job.'" He taught technical writing at a small junior college. "What's that great line? Oh, yeah . . . In Hollywood, you can die of encouragement."

"Tell me what that means to you."

He grunted. "You know damn well what it means. It means you can get better and better, everybody'll keep praising the writing, but nothin' happens. I mean, you wouldn't *believe* the response I got on my last spec. 'Best script I've read in years,' one guy said. 'Too bad they're not making relationship pictures anymore.'"

I watched as he took his seat across from me. He put his head in his hands. "It's gettin' to the point where I wish people *hated* my writing. I wish people would say, 'Give it up, asshole, your stuff sucks.' But, no . . . I've got *fans*. People who swear it's only a matter of time, that I just gotta keep at it."

"Maybe they're right. I happen to think they are."

"Yeah? Well, too bad you're not runnin' a studio." His voice thickened. "And my poor wife . . . I think she's about had it, you know? She doesn't need this shit."

"What *does* she need?"

"A husband who can wake up and smell the coffee, for

221

one thing." He leaned back in his chair, arms folded. "Let's face it. It ain't gonna happen for me, and I gotta just accept it. I just wish—"

"What?"

"This is gonna sound nuts, or egotistic or somethin' . . . but I just wish I wasn't such a good writer. I *am* good, too. And I think I'm gettin' better with each script. It's like some kinda bad joke."

At this point, I took a chance. A big one.

"Okay," I said. "Tell me what makes you so good."

"Are you shittin' me? You serious?"

"Yeah. You say you're a good writer. Based on what?"

"Based on the work." His eyes darkened, glaring at me. "I write good characters—no, *great* characters. Everybody says that, first thing. And I'm gettin' better with story, with structure. Like my last script. Character driven, no question about it, but a helluva lot of tension. You really want to know what's gonna happen to these people."

"You're right, it sounds good."

"It *is* good. And it isn't just me who thinks so." He gave me a sidelong look. "And don't think I don't know what you just did."

I smiled. "Who, me?"

"I mean, I could hear myself. It still matters. I still care." He took a deep breath. "And maybe you're right. Maybe I'm not *quite* ready to quit. Not yet. But I'm close. Believe me."

"I do."

"It's just . . ." A rueful grin. "It's just that I'm pretty damn good, ya know? That's the real pisser."

"Sure is." Now I too leaned back in my chair. "By the way, what's your next one about?"

He spent the rest of the session telling me.

Loneliness

Writing is a lonely business. It's time-consuming, frustrating, terror-inspiring, and bad for your posture. Its other prominent features include long hours of typing, frequent intervals of staring at blank pages or screens, and no guarantee whatsoever that anything you produce will be worth the effort. In addition to which, in the words of Ben Hecht, "fun is the enemy."

In fact, among the writers in my practice, the isolation and loneliness of writing is often the salient issue.

"I can't go in that room anymore," one client, a successful novelist, said to me. He worked in an office at home. "I've been going in there for fifteen years now . . . alone."

He claimed it was the sheer weight of loneliness that was taking the toll. "I keep thinking of other things I could be doing—spending time with my family and friends, being outdoors. Having a regular job."

"Do you want a regular job?"

"Hell, I don't know. It might be a relief. I mean, look at

what I do to myself. Each new book is always so life-and-death. Is it any good? Will it sell? Why am I putting myself through this?"

"Is that a rhetorical question," I asked, "or are you really wondering about it?"

"You mean, why do I do it? Keep writing? Because I *have* to . . . it's like a curse."

"Or a calling," I suggested. "When someone asked Stephen King why he writes the kind of stories he does, he answered, 'What makes you think I have a choice?'"

"Uh-huh." He slumped in his seat. "It's just lonely, that's all. In that room. I feel like the damned Maytag repairman. It's so *quiet* in there, by myself."

"It can be. But let me suggest something. Maybe you're *not* in there by yourself. Think about it. You share that room with the memory of every person you've ever encountered— your parents, teachers, friends, and enemies. . . ."

He frowned. "Listen, my office is eight-by-ten feet. If anybody *else* is skulking around in there, I sure don't see 'em."

"You know what I mean. Besides, in one sense, loneliness can mean being disconnected. Not just from others, but from your interior self. You carry a whole world of feelings, hopes, and fantasies inside you. Maybe if you let them out, and explored them fully, the office wouldn't feel so lonely."

He wasn't buying this approach. Or any other I offered.

"Okay," I said at last. "I'm with you. Writing *is* lonely. Let's say you can't go back in that room anymore. Now what?"

"What do you mean, now what? I'm gonna keep writing, I just hate the loneliness."

"Boy, I hear you."

"That's it? You *hear* me?"

"Well, you said yourself that you're going to continue

writing and you hate the loneliness. Both facts seem to coexist."

"But that *sucks*. I don't want to feel lonely writing. Or at least, I don't want to mind it so much."

"I hope you get there. Until then, ask yourself this: Can you accept both your desire to write *and* your pain of feeling lonely? As Jung might say, can you love that struggle? Not the triumph of one side or the other, but the struggle itself. Can you tolerate the tension of that?"

He grew pensive. "I don't know. That's a good question."

"And not an easy one to answer."

He just nodded.

We return to this issue again and again in therapy. Some days his loneliness overwhelms him, leaving him lethargic and unmotivated; other times a patch of solid writing makes him so excited to get back to "that room" that he actually feels lonely—in essence, disconnected—when he's *not* writing.

There's no solution to loneliness, nor should there be. It's part of the human condition, and often a component of any creative act. I believe it's finding some equanimity in the swirl of all your feelings about writing that enables you to keep at it. That all aspects of the work, even those you dislike, have the potential to inform and enlighten, if you're able to embrace them.

So whether you "love the struggle" or "feel like the damned Maytag repairman," you're being where you need to be, doing what you need to do. You're a writer.

Larry: A True Story

The last story I want to tell involves not a client, but a friend. It's a true story, though of course I've changed many of the details to protect the confidentiality of the people involved. I think it belongs in this book because it concerns a struggling writer at the end of his rope, and a last-chance interview that saves his life. It's about hard work, daring, and hope. It illustrates the ways the writing life can lift you up and crash you down. It also reaffirms my belief that good writing persists, matters, transcends.

And that every once in a great while, it can even save your soul.

Larry was an angry, wickedly funny comedy writer who came out here to Hollywood from the East Coast about the same time I did. This was the early 1970s, during the stand-up comedy boom, and he and I met one night at the Comedy Store on Sunset Boulevard. It was a Monday night, "Audition Night" at the club, so there was the usual long line of would-be George Carlins and David Steinbergs extending out of the front door and around the corner into the alley. Larry and I found ourselves standing in line between a tall black ventriloquist whose dummy sported an Afro, and a husband-and-wife comedy team who'd just arrived from Ohio and were living out of their car. Larry announced he was from Brooklyn, I said I was from Pittsburgh, he offered his condolences, and our friendship began.

To audition for the Comedy Store was a trying business. After standing in line for an hour or so, you finally reached the desk at the top of the stairs, just inside the entrance. There, a little overhead light illuminated a yellow legal pad, upon which the door guy wrote down your name. And the time you'd be performing. I got 1:20 A.M. Larry got 1:30. I looked at my watch. It was 8:15.

"Looks like we got a little time to kill," Larry said. "You hungry?"

We ate at the Hyatt Hotel coffee shop next door to the Comedy Store, spending the next couple of hours insulting the looks and probable lack of talent of pretty much every other person in the audition line. We definitely enjoyed riffing off each other's jokes and observations, though neither of us was psychologically sophisticated enough to realize how terrified we were. Two insecure, neurotic guys in their twenties who left good jobs back east to come to L.A. to become writers. Neither of us, we agreed, wanted to do stand-up comedy for a living, but everyone knew that producers and TV stars hung out at the Comedy Store all the time, looking for funny stuff they could steal and fresh new talent they could exploit. Like Larry, I yearned to join the list of the robbed and exploited.

We each did well during our audition sets, which meant

we each got some laughs and managed to stay on stage for the allotted ten minutes without getting The Yellow Light. An obvious homage to the infamous "hook" of the vaudeville days, The Yellow Light was a blazing spotlight that was trained on you in the middle of your act if the management decided you sucked beyond endurance. I used to wince whenever I saw some poor comic wanna-be impaled by that searing amber light, caught like some fugitive in a 1930s gangster movie. I always expected to hear police sirens and barking dogs.

Anyway, neither of us got The Yellow Light, which meant that we'd made it onto the roster of regular comics. What *this* meant was that the club's owner, Mitzi Shore, would draw up a schedule each week and each comic would get a fifteen-minute slot. If you were a hot comer, like Freddie Prinze or Jimmy "JJ" Walker, your slot was usually eight or nine o'clock on a Friday or Saturday night. If you were a slug like me, you were lucky to get 1:15 A.M. on a Tuesday.

I did a lot of those late-night gigs, playing to an audience of waitresses, busboys, the two comics who were waiting to go on after me, and a couple drunks. I felt as though I lived in an episode of *The Twilight Zone,* one of those melancholy, *noir*-like stories with Jack Klugman or Ross Martin wandering a dark alley, wearing a dead guy's raincoat. The only other comic who got as many bad time slots as me was some kid from Indiana named David Letterman. Though I hear he's gone on to do pretty well for himself.

Larry and I compared notes during this period, each of us writing TV sitcom scripts on spec, trying to get an agent interested. I'd met and begun working with a writing partner by then, a guy named Mark Evanier, since it seemed easier to break in that way. Plus, since Mark was a lot funnier than me, our spec scripts had better jokes.

Like me, Larry soon tired of going nowhere as a comic and drifted away from regular performing at the club. He wanted to concentrate solely on his writing. I, on the other hand, still dutifully trudged up on stage once or twice a week, sometimes getting slots as juicy as 10:30 on a Thursday night. The truth is, some adolescent, deluded part of me was still waiting to be "discovered."

Which, in a way, I was. One night, after performing a pretty good set, Gabe Kaplan, star of the ABC-TV series *Welcome Back, Kotter,* came up to me and said he was interested in hiring a writer for when he went back on the road. Like many comics starring in hit shows, during vacations and breaks in the shooting schedule, Gabe did his stand-up act in clubs and hotels around the country. He told me that night that he'd call me about writing some new material for him. I went home elated, ecstatic.

He was true to his word. Eleven months later, he called on a Friday, offered me $250 a week to travel with him and work on his act, and told me we had to leave the next day. Of course, I jumped on it.

It was this experience that led, seven months later, to my partner, Mark, and I being offered a job on the writing staff of *Welcome Back, Kotter.* Which was the lucky break that started my career as a Hollywood writer.

Over the next ten or fifteen years, as a solo writer, I worked on numerous TV series and films. I had my ups and downs, like every other writer I knew, but on the whole, things worked out pretty well for me.

I wish I could say the same for Larry. I've never known

anyone who suffered so much trying to become a success as a writer. He wrote dozens of spec scripts, and a few screenplays as well. He sweated out every scene, labored over every joke. But his luck was bad. He'd get a producer interested in a script, but the guy would change his mind right before signing a deal. He'd pitch a series idea to a network, and they'd develop it with another writer. Once, in desperation, Larry worked fourteen hours a day for five months, hammering out a novel that he eventually sold—to a publisher that went out of business six weeks later.

On top of all this, Larry had romantic troubles, physical ailments, bouts of debilitating depression, and a growing reputation as an angry, bitter, cynical guy. His years of struggle had taken their toll on his ability to muster much optimism, or general good feeling at all. At lunch with fellow writers, he'd complain so much about the state of the writing business that, after a while, nobody wanted to have lunch with him. The few times he'd land a writing job—say, nine weeks as a staff writer on a low-rated sitcom—he'd so infuriate the show's producers with his continual putdowns and insults that his contract was never renewed. Larry's self-loathing radiated out to ensnare those around him, to the extent that one mutual friend said to me, "Show business is tough enough without having to listen to *his* shit."

After a dozen or so years of scraping by, borrowing rent money from friends and family (and even, one time, from his agent!), Larry was hospitalized for severe depression. His girlfriend left him, his landlord evicted him, and his agent stopped returning his calls.

Then his life turned bad. A series of serious illnesses befell him, leaving him with ulcers, a back constantly in pain, and failing eyesight. He gained weight, lost a lot of his hair, and alienated most of his friends. He also began drinking and smoking heavily.

During all this, Larry kept trying to write. He'd get me on the phone and talk for hours about some new screenplay he was working on, or some new series idea he wanted to sell. His writing, as always, was infused with bitterness and a kind of pervasive misanthropy, but it was also funny. His characters, either broadly comic or obviously craven, belonged, in the view of many, to a style of Hollywood storytelling that had vanished. And, when pitching, if there was a way to guarantee angering the potential buyer to such an extent that he'd never want to meet again, Larry could do it. (Often, he'd open a pitch to a producer or network exec by suggesting that they could use a great new show, given the crap they currently aired. In Larry's mind, this was just "telling it like he saw it.")

Once, during this period, when he was so broke he was sleeping on the couch in a distant cousin's mobile home, an old friend pulled some strings and got Larry a single episode of a waning Norman Lear sitcom. Somehow, through the rage and the bourbon, Larry pushed himself to crank out the script. And it was good. Funny. He'd really nailed it.

The show's producers were thrilled. Larry was thrilled. There was talk of offering him more episodes, maybe a job on the writing staff. Things were finally turning around.

Then the show got cancelled.

Larry sort of unraveled after that. A new agent who'd been interested lost interest. Other hoped-for writing jobs either failed to materialize, or went south due to personality conflicts, or were illusory to begin with. Larry started drinking more, smoking more, sleeping less. His health, as if this were possible, got even worse. His shrink was forced to hospitalize him again.

Finally, after sixteen years in Hollywood, Larry came to a decision. When I saw him at a coffee shop soon after he got out of the hospital, he told me that he was going home. Back to Brooklyn. He was giving up.

A few weeks later, having sold his precious books for traveling money, he climbed into his beat-up Ford Torino station wagon and headed east.

We heard stories about him from time to time. That he'd gotten into huge fights with his family back in New York and had moved upstate. The occasional postcard announced he was working at a deli somewhere, or selling T-shirts at Mystic Seaport, or tutoring high school kids in New Haven.

Then, a couple years later, I learned that Larry had gotten married and had a kid. He was working in a factory in some small town in New Hampshire. His father back in Brooklyn had died, his mother had moved in with his sister, and, apparently, nobody was speaking to anybody.

Then, the final blow: Larry's wife was diagnosed with the early signs of Parkinson's disease. She lost her job at the library and needed her mother's help with the baby. Money was tighter than ever, with medical bills mounting by the week, and Larry wasn't making enough to cover them.

What happened next is the reason I wanted to tell this story. And, while true, it is the part that lifts this story to the realm of fable, to that place where the elements of life seem to exhibit a magical confluence beyond our ken.

What happened next, simply enough, was that Larry saw a notice in the paper announcing that a small college not ten miles from his apartment was looking for someone to teach TV and film writing. At first, Larry hesitated about applying for the job. For one thing, the college, though small, was amply endowed and quite well-respected for its liberal arts programs. For another, Larry wasn't a teacher. He'd tutored high school kids, but held no educational credentials. He'd graduated with a Master's in English from Brooklyn College, but then, as he'd once said, "who didn't?"

There was no way, he thought, that he'd qualify for the job. So, naturally, Larry being Larry, he applied for it.

On the day of the interview, Larry was a wreck. He'd stared dumbfounded at a mountain of bills the night before. His infant son had colic and had been screaming since dawn. His wife, growing ever weaker from the ravages of the disease, had urged him to consider their moving in with her parents.

Regardless, Larry got himself to the office of the Dean of the TV and film department. Sitting across from the stereotypically tweedy academic, whose desk was littered with texts and papers and knickknacks, Larry gave the performance of his life. He talked about his years in Hollywood, his toils in the vineyards of writing, his real-world experience and its value for his prospective students. And, aside from a few cracks he couldn't resist making about what dimwits and sycophants the entertainment industry attracted, Larry came off as reasonably amiable.

The Dean remained unimpressed. He made some polite noises about appreciating Larry's enthusiasm and desire and even acknowledged that Larry's show business experiences were something most other applicants for the job lacked. But it just didn't seem likely that a person without any teaching credentials would be suitable for the position.

"I mean," said the Dean, "you haven't developed a curriculum, you don't know the standard texts we use . . . I'm afraid, frankly, that we wouldn't be the best place for you."

The Dean went on to compliment Larry on the impression he'd made and added that perhaps if he went back to school and got his teaching degree, there'd be a place for him at the college. During this, Larry sank further and further into his chair, as though under the weight of all his years of rejection, all his years of failure.

And all the writing he'd done. The late nights, the rewrites, the thousands of pages pored over and corrected and revised. The hundreds of pitch meetings, the lunches with idiot producers, the pandering to moronic tastes, the arguments with agents, and on and on.

And all of it a waste. Useless. A twenty-year trek through a merciless forest that deposited him here, in this bland little guy's office, in this small college town, ten miles down the road from the dreary apartment where his ailing wife and needy baby waited. A family burdened by illness and debt, and a husband and father who was powerless to do anything about it.

Larry's eyes filled with tears. He sat unmoving in the chair, as the Dean was winding up his speech. The little man was trying to be kind, but after all, Larry wasn't really qualified for the job. . . .

The Dean was coming around from behind his desk now, extending his hand. Larry knew he should get up, get to his feet, shake the man's hand . . . but somehow he couldn't do it. Couldn't move.

As the Dean came around the desk, he accidentally knocked a thick textbook onto the floor. On impulse, Larry bent down to pick it up. And froze.

The Dean noticed this, and gave Larry an odd look.

Larry pointed down at the book, which had fallen open somewhere in the middle.

"What is this?" Larry managed to say, though he was having a hard time forming words.

"The book? It's our standard first-year text. On TV scriptwriting."

"TV writing?"

"Why, yes. There are samples from produced scripts, writing exercises. You know."

"Yes," Larry said. "I *do* know."

He picked up the book and showed the opened page to the Dean. Indicating with a finger, Larry read a passage from the book praising the sample TV script used in this particular lesson. The reprinted scenes were considered classic examples of sitcom pacing, structure, and humor derived from character.

"Do you know these scenes?" the Dean asked.

"Yeah," Larry answered. "I wrote them."

The Dean stared over Larry's shoulder at the opened pages. The TV script that the textbook used as an example of the best of its kind was Larry's one script he'd done for the Norman Lear sitcom years before.

When the Dean looked up from the book, he saw the tears rolling down Larry's cheeks. And in that moment, the Dean did something neither he nor Larry could have ever predicted.

He offered Larry the job, right on the spot.

In the succeeding years, Larry became one of the school's most well-respected teachers. He also became embroiled in faculty politics, made his usual quotient of enemies, and generally became a "character" on campus. He wrote scathing pieces in the local paper about state politics, the sorry situation in higher education, and his overall dissatisfaction with just about every element in contemporary life. He debated students in lecture halls, colleagues in faculty lounges, and townspeople in bars.

He was, in short, happy.

Today, whenever he tells the story of what happened that day in the Dean's office, Larry refers to it as the time when his writing saved his life. When a nearly forgotten script, the product of years of struggle and misfortune, of rejection made only the more painful by momentary glimmers of hope, reached out of the past as though with a will of its own to validate him.

Earlier in this book, I maintained that a writing career required the same commitment, the same degree of hard work, perseverance, and love, as any important relationship in our lives. And that sometimes, similar to other relationships, it can feel like *we're* doing all the giving.

Larry's story demonstrates that once in a while, in ways you can rarely predict, writing gives something back. Not just a job, or a second chance. Not even some kind of testimony to all the labors you've endured in its behalf.

What writing can give you, to the extent to which you use it as a vehicle for self-knowledge, self-expression, and intimate communion with the deepest regions of your interior world, is a glimpse of the truth. Writing can be a two-way mirror into your soul, an ongoing process of discovery and growth.

Every word you write is precious, regardless of its power, eloquence, or viability. It's the concrete symbol of the continuing expression of your subjective experience, offered to yourself and others, in the hopes of making a connection, of uncovering the things that bind each person to every other person, that makes us human.

Just as, one day in the office of a small liberal arts college, something that Larry had written years before created a bridge between his past and his present, and between himself and the Dean, so too can your writing surprise, inform, delight, and amaze you with its ability to make connections.

So too can your writing, if you're willing to let it, be the daily practice of the art of being yourself, and the ultimate pathway to the awareness that you—just as you are—are enough.

Conclusion

*In the beginner's mind, there are many possi-
bilities; in the expert's mind, there are few.*

SHUNRYU SUZUKI

It all boils down to this:

1. Every successful writer started out as a struggling one.
2. Even the successful ones still struggle.

Every day in my private practice, I see clients who refuse
to accept the foregoing maxims. Writers embedded in a creative hell of their own making, in the grip of self-shaming
and self-defeating meanings about who they are and what
they deserve, are almost incapable of acknowledging that
the problems they suffer with their work are the same as
those suffered by writers everywhere. The underlying causes
of their misery, procrastination, and blocks, their fears of

failure and sense of themselves as intrinsically defective, may vary from writer to writer, but the painful feelings that accompany the writer's life are known to all.

What makes this notion so difficult to accept? I can think of a number of reasons: If there is indeed something wrong with us, then there's the possibility that someone, somewhere, knows how to fix it; if we can somehow be different from who we are, we won't be plagued by these painful, debilitating feelings; if everybody struggles, regardless of professional success, then we have to abandon our hopes that if *we* attained such success, our personal and creative difficulties would disappear.

For me, both personally and professionally, the awareness that *all* writers struggle daily with their art, with the balance between the demands of work and life, is a source of comfort. It means I don't have to be so damned special to write. I don't have to overcome, or transcend, things about myself to do good work.

Moreover, I'm in the same game as everybody else, bound by the same rules, gifted with similar pains and joys, flashes of insight and bouts of insecurity. As a writer and therapist, I've been both intuitive and clueless, creatively agile and artistically lead-footed. Sometimes in the same day. Sometimes in the same hour.

As have the writers I've loved and admired my whole life. Just as faith has little meaning without doubt, and courage little valor without fear, so too does writing have little impact without being an expression of the very creative and personal difficulties out of which it emerged.

If, as I've argued throughout this book, you are enough, then wherever you're at, moment to moment, becomes the crucible out of which your writing flows. Accessing this subjective space, and wedding its range of colors with craft and perseverance, is the writer's daily job.

It's what struggling, unpublished, and unproduced writers do—when they're writing well. It's also what successful, published, and produced writers do—when they're writing well. No difference.

In the end, there's just you and your writing. As screenwriter Fredrick Raphael said, when defining what he meant by work, "It's having pages in the evening that weren't there in the morning."

You. And your writing. That's all there is. That's all there needs to be.

So go. Write.